The Arab Revival

Francesco Gabrieli

The
Arab
Revival

 Random House · New York

Contents

The Glorious Past

The Glorious Past

No history of arab revival, even the briefest, can be written without some knowledge of the state from which the Arabs have fallen and to which it is their nature to rise again. A preliminary record of the great achievement of the Arabs in history and of the time and manner of their decline is therefore necessary. I shall rapidly survey the great period of the Middle Ages in order to make clear the form of Arab nationality in the past, and the relation, often far from clear to the layman, between the ethnic and national consciousness of the Arabs and their religion, Islam.

The earliest pre-Islamic history of the Arabs already shows us that this people, still shut up within its own peninsula and filtering slowly into the bow of the Fertile Crescent, had a rudimentary but clear national consciousness. Though surrounded by great Oriental or Hellenistic-Roman states, far richer and more complex in their material and spiritual life, the Arabs distinguished themselves then and thenceforward from Greeks, Romans and Byzantines, from Aramaeans and Persians, with an awareness and a national pride which found expression mainly in their poetry, the sole document of their spiritual life that has come down to us from that time, and in the historico-legendary traditions which did not aquire their final written form until somewhat later, in the first age of Islam. In these the *Arabs* distinguish themselves from the *Ajam* or non-Arabs, and more specifically from the *Fars* and the *Rum*, that is to say the Persians and Byzantines, who were their closest neighbours in the centuries before Mohammed, even as in classical civilization the Hellenes distinguished themselves from the Barbarians.

A lively sense of independence and liberty was characteristic of the Arab people, along with the usual defects of these virtues, factionalism and anarchy. Aided by the desert this sense helped to repel every invasion and attempt at foreign conquest, but it also helped to prevent the formation of sound and durable

9

political groupings. The history of the Arab peoples during the pagan period, or *Jahiliyya* shows this proud national consciousness and this inability to submit to any sort of organized authority higher than that of the tribe: the only significant exceptions to this rule were the little dynastic states, acting as buffers, which were formed in the north-east and north-west of the Arabian Peninsula, within the orbit of the Sassanid and Byzantine Empires.

On this disorganized mass of tribes, recalcitrant to every political unity but none the less conscious of common ties of race, language and primitive culture, the revelation and mission of Mohammed acted as a catalyst that united them, at least momentarily, in a single great endeavour and released a flow of formidable energy. Islam as proclaimed by the Prophet of Mecca certainly renounced the idolatrous pride of the *Jahiliyya* but, at least in its early years (and, according to some historians, for the whole life of the Founder), it revealed itself as an *Arab* faith with its own *Arab* Sacred Book, the greatest justification on the religious plane of the Arab nation. Till then they had been deprived of a divine message; now they were raised to the level of other peoples (the 'Peoples of the Book') who already possessed a sacred scripture, and to an equal dignity of relation with the One True God.

The religion of Mohammed was at first felt by the Prophet himself to be an Arab version of monotheism, of that faith which other peoples had received through the labours of other prophets, his forerunners. Far from being repudiated, the Arab national factor was exalted and formed the basis of the new faith, only the cruder and grosser excesses of racial pride being condemned. It is difficult to gather precisely how this original national conception of Islam overflowed into universalism, and it is even uncertain whether such a process can have been clearly apparent to Mohammed himself. None the less, we see it already in action soon after his death. It underlies the great movement of the Arab *diaspora*. The Arabs rushed out of their Peninsula to conquest, a people chosen by God to make His law known to the infidels, and at the same time to enjoy the

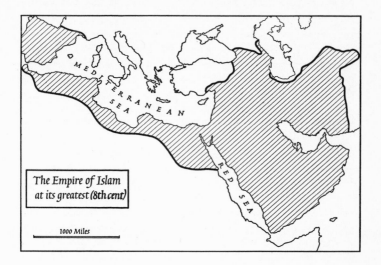

The Empire of Islam
at its greatest (8th cent)

1000 Miles

worldly benefits to which their privileged position entitled
them—'the prime material of Islam', as the Caliph Omar
called them.

Arab nationalism and Moslem universalism thus proceeded
in step for some time, fused in a single whole and unaware of
the innate contradiction which was later to make them opposed
to one another. The gigantic edifice of the Empire which arose
in the course of the seventh century as a result partly of warrior
valour and partly of luck, of improvisation and organizing
ability, of virtues and vices religious, political and civil, rested
for almost a century on this unstable compromise.

It is not necessary to recall in detail the very rapid and
remarkable extension of the Arab conquests in those early years.
Within a century of the death of Mohammed his successors at
the head of the Moslem Community, the Caliphs, ruled from
Damascus a state that stretched from the Atlantic and Spain to
the steppes of Central Asia, from Armenia to Nubia. The

governing class of this state was, during that period, entirely made up of Arabs who had brought with them from Arabia their tribal structure, with its jealousies, hostilities and squabbles, though tempered by the egalitarianism of Islam and subordinated to the central authority of the Caliphate. This supreme Islamic magistrature was and always remained in Arab hands, those of the Quraish, the Meccan tribe of Mohammed; and after the first four Caliphs, the 'well-guided' ones of the first patriarchal phase of the Caliphate, the title passed hereditarily through two dynasties, the Omayads (662–750) and the Abbasids (750–1258).

The century of the Omayads was the golden age of Arab power, the maximum expansion of an 'Arab Empire'. The effective authority of the Caliph, i.e. his power of nomination and dismissal of provincial governors, stretched from the centre of Syria to its most remote confines; in the first half of the eighth century Spain and Africa, Transoxiana and Sind still obeyed the direct orders of the Caliph in Damascus.

The Arabs however did not have any clear consciousness of living in a golden age. Such consciousness was obscured on the one hand by the enmities of particular groups, only just restrained by devotion to the central authority and the common cause, and on the other by the conflict between their national pride as Arabs and the supranational spirit of Islam, a spirit which was naturally strongest in the subjugated non-Arab masses, but which also influenced pure-blooded Arabs themselves. Both these sources of discord are apparent in the great internal crisis that in the middle of the eighth century cast down the Omayad Caliphate and substituted for it the rival Abbasids. The Abbasids were equally Arabs, but they were supported in large measure by non-Arab elements of the Empire (above all, Persian) and Moslem universalism, rather than national feeling, lay behind their ideas and methods of government. Thus the violent transfer of power from the Omayads to the Abbasids, though it in no way signified, at least in its first years, a cultural and social decline, marks the end of the political leadership of the Arabs and the break-up of their great united Empire. Spain broke away almost immediately, forming a separate state under a transplanted branch of the Omayads, followed rapidly by all Africa west of Egypt and, to the east, the farther regions of Persia and Central Asia. After less than a century of continuing power and splendour the age of the Abbasids was, in fact, marked by the progressive liquidation of the united Empire that had been created in the epic times of conquest. In none of these lands did Islam, as a religion, lose its influence; it has even extended it down to modern times; but the Arabs were no longer its exclusive apostles nor did any Arab state ever again include within its borders all the Moslem lands.

This ebb in their political power which the Arabs suffered in the middle of the eighth century, in contrast to their extraordinary outburst in the seventh was, however, largely compensated for by a wonderful cultural upsurge which culminated in this same Abbasid epoch. Just as the breaking-up of the central state and the formation of the cultural unity of Hellenism were both products of the immense Empire of Alexander, so in the Abbasid Empire, its bounds reduced little by little, and surrounded by a multiplicity of vassal or independent states that had branched off from it, Arab-Moslem civilization celebrated its greatest triumph. The term Arab-Moslem means that this culture retained some features of its pure Arab origin, primarily the language, but that the people were no longer purely Arab. The faith of Islam was now decisively universalistic in all its aspects—theological and juridical, philosophical and mystical—while the Hellenistic and Oriental cultures of the newly conquered lands penetrated the new Moslem society in Arab guise. Each of these non-Arab cultures and traditions had their vigorous champions (the so-called *Shu'ubiyya*, that is to say, anti-Arab polemists who reaffirmed the values of the 'Gentiles'), but it is characteristic that the polemic was carried on exclusively in the Arabic language. The religious, scientific and cultural primacy of Arabic remained unchallenged, even when Persian and later Turkish exerted their literary influence in Moslem lands. The Arabs in fact regained in the cultural field the leadership that they had lost in the political. Perhaps they would have lost it just the same, even without the Abbasid revolution, because of the impossibility of maintaining for long a unified Empire and an ethnic supremacy over the whole area of their Empire.

Contemporaries were aware of this change of values from a political to a religious and cultural hegemony, and judged it somewhat differently from modern historians who are accustomed to see everything from the point of view of nationalism. In fact the national sentiment, that had been so marked in the pre-Islamic Arabs and in the first period of Islam, was thenceforward thinned away more and more under the force of Islamic religious feeling, which has always bluntly condemned racial pride. So, from a Moslem viewpoint, the Omayad period appears as a 'lay' and impious government of tyrants, who disregarded the values of the faith, which only the subsequent 'blessed dynasty' of the Abbasids restored to honour. Regret for the lost Arab hegemony which was voiced only in some isolated verses of the early Abbasid era, and the sense of nationality were swallowed up in the new sense of religious and cultural unity.

The Omayads who had numbered amongst them great names and sovereigns (Muawiya, Abd al-Malik, Hisham) and had directed the imperial expansion, had failed in the task of reconciling the supremacy of the Arab people with the egalitarian universalism of Islam, sovereign authority with the independence of the tribes. The Abbasids, who resolved these contrasts by sacrificing the national to the religious principle and individualism to absolutism, also had a brief golden age, associated with the names of al-Mansur, the legendary Harun-al-Rashid and his son al-Mamun (eighth and ninth centuries), but their effective authority soon fell into the hands of court intriguers while their bureaucratic and badly administered state was involved in bankruptcy and in serious economic and social disorder. But during the very long life of the Abbasid Caliphate, which lasted up to the middle of the thirteenth century—and was moreover distinguished by an intense cultural life—there flourished other Arab or Arabized states, independent in fact and sometimes also in name, that deserve, even more than the waning Caliphate, to be recorded in the annals of the Arabs.

Iraq, where the Abbasids had from the very beginning founded Baghdad as the new capital of the Empire, remained under their direct rule or the rule of those who little by little came to hold them in tutelage. Syria, having lost the position of primacy that it had had under the Omayads, no longer knew any rule that was pure Arab save some short-lived emirates, such as that of the Hamdanids in the tenth century, the worthy adversaries of the Byzantines. But in Egypt and to the west of Egypt, in the Maghreb and in Spain, there arose in the Middle Ages great Arab states, illustrious for their power and civilization, freed from every link with what remained of the Caliphate of Baghdad. Such were primarily the heretic Fatimid anti-Caliphs of Egypt, the most outstanding Moslem dynasty that ever reigned on the banks of the Nile, who in the tenth and eleventh centuries were an essential factor in Mediterranean history and set in motion a magnificent surge of art and culture (Arab Sicily was at least nominally subject to Fatimid Egypt).

The greatest period of the Fatimids coincides with that of the other great Arab state of the West, the restored Omayad Caliphate of Córdova, which for more than two centuries united all Moslem Spain, attacked and faced Christian Europe from the West and formed the background to the great age of Arab-Andalusian civilization. After its fall at the beginning of the eleventh century, Moslem Spain broke up into a number of petty emirates (the *reinos de Taifas*) which influenced the whole eleventh century and led to the greatest expansion of its exquisite culture. Then control over Spain, as also over a great part of Northern Africa, passed to rulers of Berber stock, but completely Arabized, the Almoravids (Murābti) and the Almohads (Muwāhhadi), and with them Arabo-Spanish civilization had its last splendid glories before being extinguished, save for the long survival of Granada, by the advance of the Christian reconquest.

The Berbers just referred to represent the indigenous

element of Northern Africa with whom the Arabs had come
into contact and whom they had converted to Islam and
culturally if not ethnically absorbed. At the opposite end of the
diaspora, to the east, the Arabs came into contact with another
ethnic element, the Turkish, destined to have an even greater
effect on their history. While the Persians, after having
fomented and sustained the Abbasid revolution and having
held for a short time a position of primacy in the Baghdad
Caliphate, withdrew into their own confines and there developed
an autonomous political and cultural life under the aegis of
Islam, the barbarian Turks of Central Asia, converted to Islam
by the Arab conquest, ended by permeating the whole Arabo-
Islamic society of the East. This process commenced in the
ninth century and went on uninterruptedly in the following
centuries until the final incorporation of the Arabs into the
framework of the Ottoman Empire.

But before this conclusion was reached, Arabo-Turkish
relations were varied and complex. The Turks progressively
penetrated into the military structure of the Caliphate, and then
of the states which had broken away from it or taken its place,
until they were able to found their own Turkish dynasties and
states, the population, language and culture remaining Arab
but the ruling class being Turkish. Parallel to this process and
closely allied to it was the rise of military feudalism—a structure
that was completely new to the Arab-Islamic state, and
coinciding with growing Turkish influence. Its essential
feature was the bestowal by the sovereign of a tract of land in
non-hereditary benefice (*iqtà*) against the obligation on the
beneficiary to provide a specific contingent to the army in
times of war.

It was these Turkish military dynasties and this feudal
structure that the Crusaders found superimposed on the Arab
populations of Syria and Mesopotamia when they began their
adventure at the end of the eleventh century. It is significant
that the great champions of Islam in the defence and later in the
counter-offensive against the Franks were almost all of non-
Arab stock, Turks like Zenghi and Nuredin, later the Mameluke

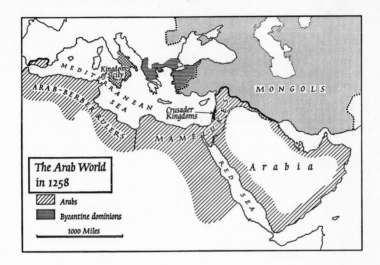

The Arab World
in 1258

▨ Arabs
▤ Byzantine dominions
1000 Miles

Baibars and greatest of them all, the Kurd, Saladin. Saladin besides being the vigorous adversary of the Crusaders, was the founder of that Ayubite dynasty and state, completely Arab in culture and in civil administration, but Kurdo-Turkish in its executive and military institutions, which held the Crusaders in check in Palestine and Egypt and made possible the union of Syria and Egypt which was the most lasting heritage of the subsequent Mameluke period.

By the twelfth century the Moslem Orient no longer knew any great Arab state, as far as the ethnic origin of the ruling dynasty was concerned, save for the Caliphs of Baghdad, now deprived of all authority; but both the Ayubites and the Mamelukes could really be considered Arab since the majority of their subjects, and therefore the language and the dominant culture of their lands, were Arab (the Ayubites also held a partial sovereignty over the Arabian Peninsula, for a long time past outside the main currents of history). The state of the

17

The Arab Revival

Egyptian Mamelukes, who about the middle of the thirteenth century took the place of the Ayubites and maintained themselves there up to the early sixteenth century, may be considered the last independent Arab state that arose from the *disjecta membra* of the ancient Caliphate, though in the veins of their Turkish and Circassian sultans there flowed not a single drop of Arab blood. In 1258 the Mongols had finally destroyed the last traces of the Caliphate and incorporated devastated Iraq, once the seat of the brilliant Abbasid civilization, into their Persian dominions. To the west of Egypt, North Africa was then divided between various Arab-Berber descendants of the Almohads, such as the Hafsids in Tunis and the Merinids in Morocco, all completely absorbed in struggles between themselves and in their relations with the Christian states of the Western Mediterranean and utterly indifferent to the fate of the Arabs of the East.

Summing up, the Arabs in their classic period emerge unexpectedly from the obscurity of the deserts; they conquer and organize a gigantic Empire during the seventh and eighth centuries, which is soon checked and reduced to fragments. There was a nucleus in the Fertile Crescent which little by little became weaker and poorer, and a series of peripheral states, some of considerable, if passing, power.

Considerably deeper and more lasting than their political fortune was the great medieval culture that they imposed on the lands conquered by them, and which forced Arab language and thought on the most varied peoples. It celebrated its greatest triumphs in Iraq in the ninth and tenth centuries, in Egypt from the tenth century onwards (this country gathered up the heritage of Iraq as the cultural centre of the whole Arab world), and in Spain from the tenth to at least the thirteenth century. This rich culture and civilization was essentially urban from the time of the Abbasids onwards, although the most ancient traditions of the Arabs were nomadic and of the desert; and in the tension between bedouin nomadism and sedentary civilization the great Tunisian thinker of the fourteenth century, Ibn Khaldun, formulated a theory of the rhythm of history in

North Africa, equally applicable to the whole Arab world of the East. The gradual and partial transformation of the bedouin to town-dwellers, their mingling with the pre-existing non-Arab populations, the combination of their original spiritual values (primarily language and poetry) with those of the Islamic faith and of ancient heredity, are the bases upon which the complex Arab-Islamic society and civilization of the Middle Ages arose. In its own eyes, as it appears to us from writings of the time, it felt itself to be *Islamic*, universalistic—a civilization in the spirit of the religion which, far beyond Arabia and the Arab peoples, was and still is the form of life for a great part of humanity. But, notwithstanding, ancient Arab pride, which had been partially subordinated to Islam, still flared up in significant expressions of haughtiness, and later of bitterness and regret. For centuries it was dominated by foreign powers, though never entirely subdued. Now, in modern times, we have seen it re-awaken.

Such in outline is the rich patrimony of the past, the consciousness which is at the root of the modern Arab revival. But before beginning to climb once more up the slope, the Arabs had to undergo a long and painful decline.

Turkish Conquest and Domination

Turkish Conquest and Domination

THE TERMINOLOGY OF WESTERN HISTORY, when applied to the history of the Arabs, has to be rearranged thus: pre-Islamic Antiquity, Renaissance, Middle Ages, modern times. The first centuries after the appearance of Islam released and expanded the Arabs' richest and most fruitful energies. But this great epoch, in which the brief political hegemony of the Arabs was followed by a longer cultural exuberance, was succeeded by inevitable decadence.

Its first symptoms can already be noted after the year 1000 and coincide with the arrival of the Turks from the East, who in the twelfth century under the Seljuk sultans officially assumed guardianship of the Abbasid Caliphate, while in the West the Arabs lost Sicily and began their long retreat from Spain. In the thirteenth century too, Arab, as well as Persian Islam, had to endure the catastrophic invasions of the Mongols which, among other things, destroyed the last vestiges of the Caliphate; and the defence against the Crusaders was mainly carried on by the Turkish element. The growth of Turkish power was the last instance of Islamic vitality before modern times; but it was the Arab peoples who paid the price for it.

The fifteenth and sixteenth centuries, the time of the Renaissance in Europe, saw in the East the final twilight of the Arab world. Its centre was transferred from exhausted and barbarized Iraq to Egypt and Syria, united under the two successive dynasties of the Mamelukes (1250–1517).

The Mamelukes did not come straight from Central Asia, as did the Turks during the Abbasid and Seljuk periods, but from nearer the West, where the Turkish *diaspora* came to a halt, especially from the shores of the Black Sea, the Caucasus and southern Russia. From these regions came the regular flow of slaves which filled the ranks of the Ayubite guard. Following a time-honoured tradition, these 'pretorian' guards gradually raised themselves to the top of the military and state hierarchy.

Their accession to supreme power was accomplished either through violence, or the consent of their companions-in-arms, or else was due to a dynastic principle which gave the first series of the new Sultans (the *Bahri* or *Nile* Mamelukes, A.D. 1250–*c.* 1390) a fairly long, continuous line of descent. On the other hand, the continuity of the second line of *Burji* or *Rock* Mamelukes, lasting from 1390 to 1517, was somewhat more interrupted.

These Turks and Circassians were rough soldiers: their education was often purely military, and sometimes they could not even speak the language of their subjects. None the less, their dominion in Egypt and its annexe, Syria, marked a final phase in the history of the Arabs of the Middle East, in which the latter's political independence, economic and cultural activities were safeguarded for them, even though they were under the sway of a foreign oligarchy.

As the Mamelukes continued to come into Egypt from the Black Sea for a long time they never forgot their native language. They brought Turkish and Persian institutions, customs and titles into military and court usage. But they always kept Arabic as the cultural language, they encouraged Arab literature and science, and were deeply conscious of the independence of their Arab domains which they defended. They were the saviours of the Near East from the Mongols, and the destroyers of the Christian states in the Holy Land. When the last vestiges of the Latin world in the Middle East disappeared (Acre in 1291, the Isle of Ruad off the coast of Tartus in 1303), Egypt and Syria were once again entirely Moslem and completely subject to the Sultans at Cairo.

The Mameluke régime was a development of military feudalism on the Seljuk pattern: temporary grants of land were made to the Emirs in return for organized military service and contributions. One of the major resources of the country had been trade with the foreigner (many commercial treaties had been preserved between the Sultans and the Latin countries, not to mention Byzantium); this was to suffer a severe blow at the end of the fifteenth century when Vasco da Gama opened up the sea-route to India by circumnavigating the Cape, and when Egypt and Syria no longer provided the usual transit road between Europe and the East.

At the same time the days of the Mameluke Empire were numbered. In contrast to the Ottoman Turks, it had been slow in learning and assimilating the results of European science, such as firearms, and this backwardness proved fatal to it in the clash with the new great Moslem power.

The spectacular development of Ottoman imperialism brought the Mameluke state to a rapid and inglorious end. A few hours of battle at Merj Dabiq near Aleppo (August 1516) destroyed their out-of-date army which scattered before the fire of the Ottoman artillery and gave Sultan Selim possession of Syria. A few months later (January 1517) Egypt fell equally rapidly, despite the defence of the valiant Mameluke Sultan, Tuman Bey, and four centuries of Ottoman dominion commenced.

Although it was frankly medieval in its structure and in its culture, this last independent Arab state had held an irreplaceable function: that of keeping the traditions of Arab culture, both in its material and spiritual aspects, which had dried up in the East, and storing it for the future. This alone makes the Mameluke régime worthy of our attention.

In the course of the sixteenth century, Ottoman power extended its pincer-movement to the extremities of the Arab world; on the east, it tenaciously contested Iraq, which had become a mere geographical expression, with the Persian Safavids, and after varying fortunes ended by taking possession of it in 1639; on the west, under the leadership of the great corsair captains, the Turks set foot in the lands of the Maghreb (in Algiers from 1516, and finally after various Spanish incursions, in Tripoli in 1551 and in Tunis in 1574), halting only on the borders of Morocco in the face of the vigorous opposition of the Sherifian state. The Turks also succeeded in penetrating into the Arabian Peninsula, leaving Morocco and the desert the only parts of the Arab world free from direct Ottoman domination.

This dominion was only more or less direct, since its effective

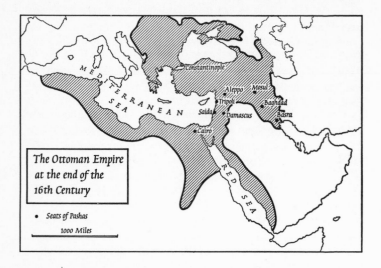

The Ottoman Empire
at the end of the
16th Century

• Seats of Pashas

1000 Miles

authority (that is, its fiscal pressure, the most evident and often the only concrete form of sovereignty in the East) varied according to time and place throughout the vast extent of the new Empire. Syria and Iraq, being the nearest to the centre, were the countries in which the government of Constantinople exercised the most continuous and direct rule through its governing Pashas (three in Syria, at Damascus, Aleppo and Tripoli, to whom a fourth, resident at Sidon, was later added; and three in Iraq, at Barsa, Baghdad and Mosul). Egypt too was ruled by a Pasha resident at Cairo with a Turkish garrison in support, though his authority was often held in check by the descendants of the Mamelukes or Beys who, though the dynasty had disappeared, continued in fact to be the great land-owners of the country, the original feudal character of the régime being attenuated and modified but not altogether abolished.

In Libya, Tunisia and Algeria, however, Ottoman sovereignty very soon became indirect, though with occasional brief reaffirmations of or attempts at more direct rule. The effective power in these lands, which Europe called the Barbary States, passed very swiftly from the nominal representatives of Constantinople to the chiefs of the militia (themselves mainly of Turkish origin and language, but much crossed with the local Arabs) and the pirate captains of the Mediterranean, since piracy was the principal occupation and source of revenue of these countries between the sixteenth and early nineteenth centuries. The Deys of Algiers, whom the French drove out in 1830, and the Beys of Tunis, who survived the protectorate of 1881 and disappeared in independent Tunisia only in 1957, stemmed from a corsair ruling class of mixed Arab, Turk and Levantine blood, who, though in formal vassalage to the Sultans of Constantinople, carried on an independent life, characterized by systematic violence, crime and plunder, until they were suppressed by Europeans. Only in Tripolitania, after a period of effective autonomy under the Karamanlis, former Turkish governors, was there a return of direct Ottoman authority between 1835 and the Italian occupation in 1912.

In these forms and in these various degrees of effective authority the Ottoman Empire held the greater part of the Arab world subject between the sixteenth and twentieth centuries. This was—for the Arabs—the saddest and most sterile period of their history, their real Middle Ages. The new masters too were faced with the dilemma that the Arabs in their hegemony had faced, the conflict between pride of race and the universalist dictates of the faith which they had embraced.

The common faith of victors and vanquished no doubt helped the latter to find foreign rule more tolerable, unlike the other subject peoples, the Greeks and the Slavs. But it is curious to note how individual Greeks and Slavs who had accepted Islam, often played a far greater part in the history of the Ottoman Empire than was ever played by the Arabs, who remained simple tributaries or, at the most, restless intermediaries between their co-nationals and the rulers, and scarcely ever rose, as did so many Ottoman subjects of Balkan origin, to the highest dignities and executive positions in the

Empire. In the most brilliant centuries of the Empire, the Ottoman ruling class counted among it Greeks, Albanians, Serbs and Bosnians (Christian peoples that the military levy on youths, and social and economic pressure, had succeeded to a great extent in Islamizing), but very few Arabs, not one of whom has left a lasting name in the annals of the Empire. Nor did the Turks make the slightest attempt, save on the eve of the final crisis of their Empire, to win over the Arabs as a people, to understand them, to alleviate their needs or to advance their material well-being or intellectual development. But it must be conceded that they treated the first-born people of Islam neither more nor less well than they treated all other peoples, Islamized or not, who fell under their unfruitful rule. They were exclusively concerned with economic exploitation and were riddled from within by venality and administrative negligence.

If one wishes to find some sort of justification for Ottoman rule, which was a typical example of misgovernment on three continents, one can only say that it distributed its evils impartially wherever it took root, and that the economic and social conditions and methods of government of the states that it supplanted were not much better—in the Arab world, for example, the hateful and oppressive Mameluke state. For *its* population the change of régime certainly did not mean any change for the worse.

The truth is that the Arab peoples, all the Arab peoples from Iraq to the extreme Maghreb, had at the time when the Ottoman rulers took over long since fallen into such a state of profound material and spiritual decadence that the loss of independence could hardly make matters worse. Living in cities seemed to have exhausted the warrior qualities of the Arabs, who owed their defence against the attacks of the Crusaders entirely to the military spirit of the Turks. Even where they remained nomads or returned to nomadism (owing to decadence of urban life in Iraq, the migratory and devastating waves of the Beni Hilal and Sulaim in North Africa in the eleventh century) the use of their arms was restricted, as it had been in pre-Islamic times, to internal tribal squabbles and plunder.

The creative period of Arab-Islamic civilization was now over: for at least a couple of centuries it had retired within itself, into crystallized social and cultural formulas. With the exception of the highly talented Ibn Khaldun (1332–1406), who however remained without a peer among his contemporaries, not an original Arabic voice had been raised in poetry, philosophy, history or science since the times of the Mongol invasions, and the always very abundant literary production was more and more limited to epitomes, commentaries and encyclopedias. The discovery of Antiquity, which was one of the stimuli of the Renaissance in the West, was lacking in Arab culture which, like the Byzantine, had always remained formally in touch with Antiquity during the European Middle Ages, but by a congenital lack of sympathy had always felt it as a sum of intellectual knowledge rather than as a humanistic education of the spirit. Arab humanism, if one may use the expression to describe the great centuries of Moslem civilization, was founded on the national poetry and the *adab*, the compendium of Arab and foreign ethics, but it had become more and more emptied of content and reduced to a trite virtuosity of courtier poets and to the most superficially anecdotic and trivial literature. Even classical Arabic, once one of its chief glories, had declined into a dead language of savants, completely abandoned in living usage for barbarized local dialects or for Turkish. The religion of Islam, too, which at one time had been the irresistible motive force of the Arab peoples, revealing in the great hours of their history their exceptional capacities and energies, had become completely fossilized in a rigid structure of orthodoxy. Only heresy and mysticism, which permeated the popular classes, remained living forces.

This decadence of the Arab world was already an accomplished fact long before the Ottoman conquest. Under Turkish rule it deteriorated almost to the point of stagnation. The Arabs accepted foreign rule, all things considered, with indifference, retaining only a vague remembrance of their former greatness; yet in the middle of the nineteenth century Kinglake noticed among the bedouin of Jordan a humbled pride as of a people 'fallen from a high estate into baseness', but this instinctive dignity had taken refuge in the primitive conditions of desert life. On the other hand, for centuries the main preoccupation of the townsfolk was to defend themselves from the avid tax-gatherers of the Ottoman authorities, and they were aided in that by the organization of corporations and guilds (in which it would however be a mistake to discern a direct precursor of modern trade unions), while the educated and cultivated *élite* escaped from the mortification of reality into literature or learning, religious edification or contemplation.

Such an attitude among the passive and impoverished masses did not, however, exclude occasional outbreaks of revolt and the kindling of autonomous movements on Arab soil during the four centuries of Ottoman domination. If Iraq, too heavily tried, still lay like a dead body throughout this period and knew no other form of social protest than brigandage, Syria and Egypt provided more than one case of rebellion, open or concealed, against the authority of Constantinople.

The best known of such movements, certainly the best known to contemporary Europe, was that of the Druse Emir of the Lebanon, Fakhr al-Din (the 'Faccardino' of contemporary Italian sources) who in the first years of the seventeenth century, relying on the hereditary power and prestige of the Ma'an family, established a personal rule over the Southern Lebanon and successfully resisted the Ottoman governors. His political plans were ambitious, and to further them, he established a connexion with the Tuscan court of the Medici. When his fortunes in his own country were at a low ebb, he actually lived in Florence for five years (1613–18), but then, returning to the East, he once again tried his luck. He reigned for some time in the Lebanon as a semi-independent sovereign, until he surrendered to the Ottoman forces and was taken as a prisoner to Constantinople where he was executed in 1635.[1]

Another great Syrian rebel, a century later, was the Lord of

---

[1] It should be noted that the Ma'an family, to which Fakhr al-Din belonged as well as its successor, the Shihab family, then exercised an autonomous hereditary power in the Lebanon, which, however, was always reconciled, save in these cases of revolt, with vassalage to the Porte and the payment of tribute.

St Jean d'Acre, Dahir, who defied the Porte in the years between 1750 and 1775. And, to pass on to Egypt, one cannot overlook the eighteenth-century precursor of Mohammed Ali, the Mameluke Sultan Ali Bey, who between 1763 and 1773 refused obedience to the sultan and set himself up as an independent lord of the Nile Valley, fighting, passing laws and building, until, after having come into conflict with his own supporters, he had to leave Egypt and was killed in an attempt to return under arms.

We have intentionally avoided calling all these 'Arab revolts', in the sense of movements of revolt and national independence, since only some of them, and those only indirectly, could really be so considered. Ali Bey, for instance, like his more fortunate imitator, Mohammed Ali, was as little Arab as the former Mamelukes from whom he derived the tradition of military despotism. Others like Fakhr al-Din, though Arab by race,[1] were more interested in personal power than in the affirmation of nationality; an ideal which may have vaguely coincided with the real reasons for their actions, but which it is a complete anachronism to isolate and emphasize.

National feeling languished in the whole Arab world during these centuries of abasement, shining only accidentally in the deeds of rebels and adventurers, who were motivated primarily by ambition, private rancour and the thirst for power and wealth. The Arabs, like all the peoples of the East, received the idea of nationality in the modern sense from Europe, and with it the connected ideas of liberty and independence. The process of learning, however, was to be a violent one. They had to learn these ideals from the Western nations who at this time were maturing and elaborating them and were later to implant them among the Eastern peoples, even while attempting hegemony and violent subjugation.

[1] The Ma'an may have been of Kurdish origin; but there is no doubt of their purely Arab culture.

The Nineteenth Century

The Nineteenth Century

THE THREE-CENTURIES-LONG LETHARGY of the Arab world was shaken by contact with the West at the beginning of the nineteenth century. Whereas in earlier centuries Europe had faced the Ottoman assaults on equal terms, she now showed herself, under Napoleon, infinitely superior technically and with a fully developed and original political and civil outlook. The Napoleonic expedition to Egypt is rightly seen as the dawn-star of new life. Indeed it might be said that the Arab world, until then still wrapped in medieval slumber, was reawakened by the tread of French feet around the foot of the Pyramids.

Metaphor apart, and without exaggerating the immediate effects of that first violent contact of the Arab world with the new Europe (effects which were over in less than three years), it remains true that it marked the start of all the subsequent spiritual and material evolution of the Arabs in the nineteenth century. The more enlightened Arabs, or the heads of Arab states, beheld thenceforward the revelation of an energetic new world, the antithesis of their traditional culture and civilization. This contact between the East and West, not in terms of power only, but also in thought and civilization became from that moment an essential factor of the modern history of the Arabs.

The nineteenth century saw the major Arab country in the Mediterranean, reawakened by Napoleon, initiating a life of its own under European influence, for all practical purposes regardless of Ottoman sovereignty. Mohammed Ali, rightly called the founder of modern Egypt, could not in any way, however, be said to have been inspired by ideals of nationalism; the harsh Albanian warrior, without a drop of Arab blood in his veins and whose mother-tongue was Turkish, was rather the last heir of the Mamelukes he had, in true Oriental style, exterminated, than the conscious champion of an Arab revival. But he had the merit of wanting to see Egypt strong, autonomous and equipped on modern European lines once he had established his rule there by the methods usual in the East. Hence his energetic drive for the reorganization of Egypt, with the aid of European advisers and instructors and the dispatch of study missions to Europe, which in a few decades set a backward and feudal country well on the way towards a more advanced economy, industry and administration.

The most evident results of technical progress under European guidance were shown in his external policy, more especially towards the old Empire to which he never denied the formal tie of vassalage. Indeed, in 1810–19, by the order and in the name of the Sultan, Mohammed Ali carried on a long and arduous campaign against the Wahhabis of Arabia (those puritans of the desert who were at that time regarded as heretical by the rest of the orthodox Moslem world), and, after that, the war of repression against the insurgent Greeks, which was only stopped by European intervention at Navarino. But when his services as a vassal did not seem to him suitably rewarded, he did not hesitate to launch his seasoned troops under the command of his valiant son, Ibrahim Pasha, against his own overlord in Constantinople.

The Egyptian campaigns in Syria and Asia Minor in 1831–2 and later in 1839–40 reversed the military situation that in 1516–17 had led to the destruction of the Mameluke state. This time it was the Egyptians, drilled and trained in the European manner (amongst others by the celebrated renegade Suleiman Pasha, formerly the French Colonel Sèves) and commanded by a man of real military talent like Ibrahim, who easily dispersed the badly armed and badly led Ottoman troops, then in the lowest state that the Empire had ever known. The fruit of these victories was the reconstituted union, for the decade 1830–40, of Syria and Egypt under the rule of Mohammed Ali, a revival of earlier and very ancient unions and a presage of others to come.

This conquest was not lasting, owing to the diplomatic intervention of the European powers who had already taken the Sick Man of the Bosphorus under their not disinterested care. Egypt had to abandon her Levantine dependency, where

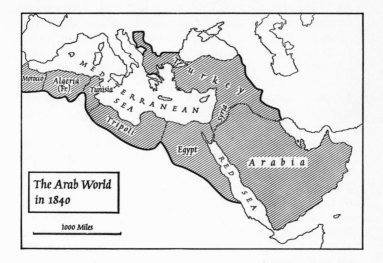

Morocco

Algeria
(Fr.)

Tunisia

Tripoli

M E D

E R R A N E A N

S E A

Turkey

Syria

Egypt

R E D

S E A

A r a b i a

The Arab World
in 1840

1000 Miles

the harsh exactions of Ibrahim had caused the first enthusiasm
for the conquest rapidly to cool. So a sense of disillusion,
bitterness and rancour clouded the last years of Mohammed Ali,
who had then to content himself (1841) with the title of Pasha
and the right of hereditary rule over Egypt, always under the
supreme suzerainty of the Porte.

Other conquests, such as that of the Sudan in 1820–3, were
more lasting; and above all, more than any acquisition of
territory, there remained the fruit that this genius of a despot
had certainly never intended, but which was none the less the
greatest consequence of his labours in peace and war: the
dawning of an Egyptian national consciousness. Now that her
soldiers had been led to victory and modernization began to
make itself felt, the country slowly began to reacquire faith in
its own military, civil and economic powers after having been
so long deprived of it. The historian of 'ifs' may well ask what
later fortunes would have been in store for Egypt had the noble

37

and intelligent Ibrahim, who was almost completely Arabized and would have been able to continue Mohammed Ali's work, not died before his father (1848). But the reaction set in after Mohammed Ali's death in 1849, with the accession of his conservative nephew Abbas and later with the more enlightened but weak Said, whose name, however, is linked with the beginning of the Suez Canal enterprise. At last, in 1863, Ismail the son of Ibrahim and a worthy successor to his grandfather, ascended the throne.

Under this ruler, who was the first to use the title of Khedive[1] which he obtained from the Porte, Egypt made further great strides on the road towards modern progress and a sense of nationality. The great public works, chief amongst them the Suez Canal (opened in 1869 during his reign) were paralleled by an intensified intellectual activity which, while it opened up Egyptian minds to the knowledge of European technical achievements, science and culture, at the same time revived the study of the Arabic linguistic and literary tradition which had till then remained somewhat neglected, with the non-Arab rulers speaking Turkish and the masses a debased dialect. In order to train teachers of the national literary language the *Dar al-Ulum* was founded in Cairo by Ismail in 1872. From this, through the interest taken in it by Ismail's son Fuad, later developed the first Egyptian university.

The weak point in the magnanimous and certainly somewhat megalomaniac activities of Ismail was the state finances, thrown out of balance by huge expenses and weighed down by debts which offered increasing opportunities for European economic and political penetration. In the first half of the century Mohammed Ali had made use of European experience and capital for the advancement of his state, but at the same time, with typical prudence and energy, he took good care to be the one to define the nature and limits of that assistance. With Ismail the scale of the penetration and the intentions of the powers concerned were profoundly changed.

Nineteenth-century Europe was then at the top of the

[1] An ancient term of Persian origin meaning sovereign or lord.

colonialist curve, a sincerely idealistic conviction of the civilizing mission of the white race mixing with the less ideal purposes of economic exploitation and political expansion. While at the inauguration of the Canal, Ismail declared that Egypt was henceforward part of Europe, the real Europe took upon itself to hasten that assimilation in quite another sense. The years 1870–80 saw the progressive domination of the financial and economic life of Egypt by the French and British, facilitated by the reckless financial policy of the Khedive (acquisition of the Egyptian shares in the Canal Company, imposition of European finance controllers, and finally the deposition of Ismail, which Europe obtained from the Porte in 1879).

In 1882, under his son and successor, Tewfik, the crisis broke. Never was European blood spilt in Africa more usefully and in a cause more welcome to Western imperialism than in the anti-foreign massacres in Alexandria in the summer of that year. They were the consequence of the long dumb discontent that had smouldered for years among the Egyptians against growing foreign interference, a discontent of which Colonel Arabi Pasha made himself the spokesman. His *pronunciamento*, aimed at imposing on the Khedive a more energetic policy of resistance to the foreigner, together with the riots and killings referred to above, gave an excuse to Britain for military intervention, and Italy and France, washing their hands, gave her a free rein. The minor skirmish of Tell el-Kebir (11th September, 1882) marked the end of the political independence of the state of Mohammed Ali (still to remain in nominal subjection to the Porte) and the beginning of British military occupation. For thirty-two years, that is until 1914, this occupation was based on a simple *fait accompli*, without any legal title even unilaterally coined, and with a disregard of international law that accumulated in the minds of the Egyptian people a fund of resentment and hatred on which even today Britain is still drawing interest.

Formally, there was no great change in the structure of the state which continued to have the Khedive (first Tewfik and then, from 1892, Abbas II) at its head, with a cabinet and a parliament; but the real executive power was in the hands of the British High Commissioner (for almost twenty-five years the energetic Lord Cromer), based on the occupation forces and the guns of the Royal Navy. So the work of Mohammed Ali and Ismail seemed to have been in vain or rather to have been turned to the advantage of the British Empire. As Kinglake had prophesied in 1834, Britain had now assured herself of a firm footing in the Nile Valley to the profit of its own finance and industry and of a guard over the Canal, the vital artery of imperial communication.

Having been blunt thus far, it remains to add in fairness that the British administration in Egypt maintained with redoubled energy the modernization and technical advancement of the country that had commenced in the early nineteenth century. It developed the great network of drainage and irrigation on which the Egyptian economy is founded, built schools and hospitals, looked after health and hygiene, communications and trade. In a word, the British carried out, with competence and efficiency, the constructive function of colonialism which should not in honesty be denied even by its most fervid adversaries. At the same time, it indirectly gave a fresh impulse to Egyptian national feeling which was bound, bit by bit, to conflict with foreign hegemony and finally to oust it from the country.

The fortunes of Syria were quite different and distinct from those of Egypt. This region then included the Lebanon and Palestine and part of present-day Jordan, and save for the decade of precarious annexation to the Egypt of Mohammed Ali, it remained an integral part of the Ottoman Empire until 1918. Here the multiplicity of races and creeds and religious communities (Maronites, Druses, orthodox Sunnis, dissident Shias, Greek Orthodox, Alouites, Jews, and Latin Christians), with their rivalries and feuds, played into the hands of anyone who wished to rule over their divided peoples, even if it formed an obstacle to close centralization. This, however, was the aim that the Porte proposed itself in the mid-nineteenth century: eliminate the intermediate powers of governors and local chiefs and reduce this confusion of peoples and faiths to a common direct dependence on Istanbul. The 'Imperial Rescript' (*Khatt-i-Humayun*) of 1856 sanctioned the legal and fiscal equality of all the subjects of the Empire contrary to the dictates of classical Moslem law. Despite its appearance of modernizing and liberalizing the Ottoman state, the real aim was to create administrative unity and to encourage patriotic feelings and direct loyalty to the Empire among the disparate ethnic elements that comprised it. As far as the Arabs were concerned, such aims were never achieved and the dualism between Arabs and Turks persisted tenaciously up to the dissolution of the Ottoman Empire.

In 1860 there were massacres of Christians in the Lebanon and at Damascus, which provoked French military intervention and led to the creation of a separate régime for Mount Lebanon (1864). It was detached from the rest of Syria and made directly dependent on the centre of the Empire. Apart from reforms and administrative rearrangements, the Lebanon and Syria, Christians and Moslems, Arabs and Turks alike, with every other subject race of the Empire during the last quarter of the nineteenth century, had to endure the levelling despotism of one of the most debased tyrants of history, the 'Red Sultan', Abdul Hamid II (1876–1909).

This cynical but extremely able man, whose only aim was to preserve his personal and absolute power and to repress by every means even the slightest breath of liberty in the peoples subject to him, maintained himself on the throne for more than thirty years, thanks to a régime of secrecy and terror. Notorious for the Armenian massacres, permitted if not ordered by him, for the abrogation of the Constitution he granted when he came to the throne, and for the elimination of the best among the Ottoman *élite*, such as the noble Midhat Pasha, Abdul Hamid could certainly have no sympathy for the Arabs of Syria, with their aspirations towards autonomy or even complete independence (we shall see these evolving in the next chapter). The break-up of the Ottoman Empire was a matter of indifference to him; his professed ideal was pan-Islamism

—his real purpose tyranny and the suppression of all liberal progress.

The Hamidian régime, with the police and censorship as its instruments, weighed especially heavily on the younger Arab generation in Syria and the Lebanon who were aspiring to a modern way of life. Many intellectuals from these countries emigrated to Egypt, where even under British occupation freer conditions flourished. Another strong current of migration, driven primarily by economic forces, went towards the two Americas, above all the United States and Brazil; and from America, from Europe and from Egypt there filtered into Ottoman Syria new ideas, and hopes and dreams of a better life.

In the meantime whatever spiritual or material progress was achieved within the country itself (public works, railways, schools) was due to foreign initiative independently, and often against the wishes, of the Ottoman authorities. A great part of these works was French. An ancient tradition dating back to the Crusades, mingling motives of political prestige, and religious and cultural missionary zeal, led her to engage herself in the Levant.

At the time, with Arab nationalism still in its infancy and oppressed by the reactionary Hamidian régime, French aid and influence was felt as a beneficent force by all the most advanced Arabs, Christian and Moslem alike, of Ottoman Syria.

Direct contact between France and the Arab world was meanwhile taking place elsewhere, on the North African coast, a region withered and wasted by centuries of Barbary rule. Whatever has happened since, the French expedition to Algiers in 1830 must be regarded as a service to civilization more important than any question of nationality, since it put an end to the worst nest of pirates in the Mediterranean. The occupation of Algiers and the other coastal centres was followed by almost twenty years of guerrilla warfare before the French obtained full possession of the country. Opinions about this war will vary, according to whether or not one recognizes the right of a superior civilization to impose itself on primitive peoples, to give them the benefits of technical progress and to take in exchange the riches which they themselves cannot appreciate, beginning with their land.

Arab resistance in the interior is famous for the noble and valorous figure of Abdul-Kader who held the French forces at bay for fifteen years and at one time even involved the neighbouring empire of Morocco (French victory at Isly, 1844) to be beaten at last only by the material superiority of the enemy. With true Arab chivalry and nobility, this same Abdul-Kader later gave refuge and safety in Damascus to Christians hunted for their lives by Moslem fanatics. Having broken the resistance of the inhabitants, France then turned to the organization and colonization of Algeria. When we now watch the drama that is drenching that land with blood, it seems almost incredible that the intense economic growth of Algeria and the influx of vast numbers of colonists should have gone on in almost complete peace[1] through the whole of the second half of the nineteenth century and the opening decades of the twentieth. These were, however, the two most serious factors leading to the present crisis.

Fifty years after Algiers came the turn of Tunisia. In the Middle Ages this country had been a flourishing and civilized state under the Hafsids, but had decayed under Barbary rule. By about 1880, though it could no longer truthfully be considered a nest of pirates and dangerous to the free navigation of the Mediterranean, it was by its geographical position marked down for European expansion—which was already under way with the establishment there of substantial communities of Europeans, mainly Italians. Franco-Italian rivalry for the right of intervention in Tunisia, and the repercussions of the French *coup* on European politics are not part of the history of the Arabs. The turbulence of the Krumiri on the borders of Tunisia and Algeria provided a convenient pretext for military invasion and the harmless reigning Bey submissively signed the Treaty of Bardo (12th May, 1881) which established the Protectorate. Unlike the Dey of Algiers, who paid for his thoughtless

[1] Some local revolts, for example, in 1871 and 1881, cannot be compared either in duration or extent with that of 1955 onwards.

behaviour to the French consul with complete political elimination, the Tunisian Bey saved by this signature, not only his own dynasty, but what was of greater importance, the forms of state and nation. Though Tunisia was now taken 'under protection' it was not absorbed under direct rule, and the consequences of the two separate treaties were to be seen many years later when Algeria and Tunisia both claimed independence.

At the end of the nineteenth century, therefore, we see a great part of the Arab world still rotting within the disintegrating Ottoman Empire, and most of the other part passing under the rule of new masters; but these new masters, unlike the Turks, were more or less consciously instilling into their subjects the sense of dignity of free men.

Thus the new culture and new political ideals of the Arab world in the second half of the nineteenth century were produced by material and intellectual contact with the West. At first they only took root in the central lands, Egypt and Syria, and it was many years before similar revivals followed in the Arab borderlands. Although the two countries had very different political destinies, they have in modern times always formed a cultural unity, the real core of the Arab world. Both, although in different spheres, came into contact with the West and reacted to the impact of European civilization. Knowledge of the principal European languages, English and French, became an essential part of a good modern education for the youth of Syria and Egypt, and through these languages they were introduced to the literatures and the philosophical and political thinking of the West. For the more advanced among the Arabs the latter part of the nineteenth century was what the eighteenth century had been for Europe, the period of *Aufklärung*, enlightenment, the enrichment and broadening of their traditional culture, the opening of new horizons and the flowering of new ideals. These were, however, not born as a spontaneous creation of the Arab peoples, but were a result of fertilization by Western culture.

It will be proper to say a word here about Moslem modernism, a supranational movement, like Islam itself. One of the effects of the many contacts with the West and with Christianity (which was naturally identified with it), was the need to reinterpret and present Islam in a new form, purified and brought into line with the needs of modern life. A reply was felt to be needed to the hostile European view of Islam as an obscurantist religion incompatible with modern progress, a reaffirmation, despite the incrustations of the centuries, of its universal and eternal values—pure monotheism, direct relationship between God and man, simplicity and clarity of dogma, humanity and practicality of ethics—and a statement at the same time of the necessary connexion between this simplified and purified concept of the Moslem faith and the political revival of the peoples who professed it. Absolutism, the ancient sore of Oriental history, was, according to the Moslem modernists, in no way a necessary consequence of the faith and law of Islam. It should now, they argued, give way to more reasonable and humane forms of social life, and to democracy itself, for which some anticipation or reflection was to be found in the origins of Islam and in the Koran, but of which Europe and America then provided most positive and concrete examples. The democratic ideals of the West, associated with the rise of national states, came to be seen as equally applicable to the Islamic East and reconcilable with the preservation and revival of its religious faith.

A rejuvenated and purified Islam and a community of Moslem peoples emancipated from every external and internal servitude, ruling themselves by free representative institutions, was the ideal of the leaders of Islamic modernism in the later years of the nineteenth century. The most prominent were the Afghan or Persian propagandist Jamal al-Din al-Afghani (1838–97) and his Egyptian disciple Mohammed Abduh (1849–1905); two men of contrasting temperament, whose disinterested, saintly lives and devoted idealism were an honour to the civilization that produced them, even if it did not spare them strife, persecution and sorrow. Neither of them could be called a direct champion of the Arab national movement (the first was not even an Arab by blood, although of perfect Arab culture) but each of them was a powerful influence on its development, making the Arabs feel the dignity of their origin, the greatness of their past and the permanent values of their faith, and at the same time counselling them, as free men, to assimilate all that was best in what the European invaders offered in technical progress and political organization.

The generation which grew up in the last years of the nineteenth and at the beginning of the twentieth century felt to the full the influence of Islamic modernism, and it has persisted in changed circumstances down to our own days long after the death of its two first apostles. In addition to this trend with its accent on religious reform, there was a vigorous propaganda movement more mindful of political and social problems flourishing primarily in Egypt, but with a large participation of Syrians, in which the finest minds of the two countries took part. This was the golden age of Arab journalism, renowned for its enthusiasm for modern ideas and for number and quality of its members. Periodicals such as *al-Hilal* and *al-Muqtataf*, published in Egypt, were the intellectual nourishment of all educated Arabs of the time. Many journalists stand high in the history of Arab literature, for example the Syrians, al-Kawakibi (1849–1902), Adib Ishaq (1865–85), Neguib al-Haddad (1867–99) and Jurgi Zaidan (1861–1914), and the Egyptians, Qasim Amin (1868–1908) and Abdullah al-Nadim (1834–96), and the Turco-Arab, Wali al-Din Yeghen (1873–1921); and lest they remain names only, we can mention at least al-Kawakibi's impassioned volume *Tyranny*.

Two disciples of Jamal al-Din al-Afghani were Adib Ishaq and Abdullah al-Nadim, and the latter took an active part in Arabi Pasha's movement. Jurgi Zaidan was the typical all-round journalist of the close of the nineteenth century, an indefatigable interpreter of European thought, science and art, who in the Dumas manner recreated the past glories of the Arabs in a famous cycle of historical novels. Qasim Amin was chiefly interested in the cause of female emancipation, and his most famous book was *The Liberation of Woman*. Wali al-Din

Yeghen suffered under the odious Hamidian régime and recounted his sufferings in verse and prose. Other notable writers in the Arab Press of the time are Mohammed Abduh, for some time chief editor of the official Egyptian newspaper *al-Waqai al-Misriyya* and Mohammed Muwailihi (1868–1930) who collaborated in exile with al-Afghani and wrote biting social satires on contemporary Egypt.

The historian can still salute late-nineteenth-century Arabic journalism, the first significant manifestation of the Arab revival in the cultural even more than in the strictly political field, for its noble faith in what are usually called the ideals of the nineteenth century: liberty of the individual and of peoples, human brotherhood, enlightened progress, democracy. The Arab East took them all from the West, though the West was even then contradicting them in practice in its relations with the 'coloured peoples', Arabs included. But this practical consideration did not take from them their faith in and enthusiasm for the principles. Re-reading the pages of these writers, one often feels beneath the ornate and exaggerated Oriental style the echoes of accents familiar to us, echoes more or less direct of the voices of Rousseau and Voltaire, Mill and Hugo, Garibaldi and Mazzini.

National Aspirations up to 1914

National Aspirations up to 1914

TURNING FROM THE CULTURAL FIELD where Syria and Egypt shared a common literary and intellectual revival, to the specifically political one, we have to treat the first attempts to attain national ambitions in Egypt, now a distinct entity, separately from those in the Arab lands subject to the Ottoman Empire. Antonius's *The Arab Awakening* to which everyone has up till now referred for this period, is in fact limited to the Arabs of the Fertile Crescent, that is to say of the Ottoman provinces, and omits Egypt altogether, to say nothing of the Maghreb. When his book was written it was premature to think of a wider conception of Arab nationality or to consider larger groupings in a free Arab world.

The decisive date for the national and civil aspirations of the Arab subjects of the Ottoman Empire was 1908, the year of the Young Turk revolution which put an end to the absolutism of Abdul Hamid. Before that date no records of revolutionary movements can be found within the Empire, save for the obscure activities of some secret societies, like one which seems to have existed about 1875 with its centre at Beirut, preaching liberal and constitutional rather than national principles. Abroad, however, ideals and projects for an Arab revival naturally preceded the fall of the Hamidian régime; and it is with the publication in Paris in 1905 of a book called *Awakening of the Arab Nation in Turkish Asia* by Neguib Azuri, who seems to have been a Palestinian Arab, and who spoke in the name of 'Ligue de la Patrie Arabe', that we find traced the first plan for a great independent Arab state, stretching from Mesopotamia to the Isthmus of Suez, granting autonomy to the Lebanon and the Holy Places of Palestine, and forecasting both an Arab Sultan at its head as well as a Caliph, that is to say a 'General of Islam', to be chosen in the person of an Emir of the Hejaz. The two principles of Arab national independence (still in a geographically limited sense) and of pan-Islamic catholicity were thus stated and linked together, though in the future they were to grow further and further apart.

An active policy and propaganda for a free Arab state dates from 1908. The revolution in that year which extorted from the Red Sultan a new or renewed Constitution, and a year later finally eliminated him from political life, raised great hopes among the Arabs as among all the non-Turkish races of the Empire. Within its framework the Young Turks of the Committee of Union and Progress promised individual and collective liberty, free representative institutions, in a word, democracy. But, as might be expected, once the central tyranny had fallen, the claims of the non-Turkish races (not only Arabs but Greeks, Slavs, Armenians, Kurds) were impetuously raised, demanding a good deal more than the Young Turks were disposed to concede. They certainly agreed to grant to the Arabs in particular some civil liberties and the right of representation in parliament but not full autonomy and still less secession from the Ottoman state, whose unity the Young Turks were determined to preserve. Hence the disillusion and unrest among the Arabs after their first enthusiasm for the revolution, and hence also the uncertainty of aim that prevailed in the years between 1908 and the First World War, ranging from collaborationist programmes that did not actually demand the total secession of the Arabs from the Empire, to those who already openly preached the extreme solution.

An example of the first was the 'Association of Arab-Ottoman Brotherhood' which worked in Constantinople in the years 1908–9, and the 'Ottoman Party for Decentralization', created by Syrian *émigrés* in Egypt during the Balkan Wars of 1912 with the aim of supporting the threatened integrity of the Empire, while granting administrative autonomy to the Arab lands. Another Arab society, secret but not extremist, with a programme of Arab autonomy, indeed almost of a dual Arabo-Turkish state on the Austro-Hungarian model, was the 'Association of the Pact' (*al-Ahd*), founded in Constantinople by Abdul Aziz al-Misri, notable for being the rallying-point for many Iraqi officers who were later to play a leading part in events in Iraq after the war. But other secret groups, both within and without the Empire, already aimed explicitly at a separatist programme; such was the Qahtaniyya group, of *carbonaro* and masonic type, which was swelled by many Arab officers of the Empire, and in Paris the 'Young Arab Association' called also, more briefly, 'The Young' (*al-Fatat*) which was led, in France and later in Syria, by Syrian and Lebanese intellectuals. These and other similar groups openly discussed one or more quite independent Arab states, freed from every tie with Constantinople.

A still relatively moderate and collaborationist attitude was taken by the Arab Congress of Paris in 1913, officially convened on the initiative of the 'Decentralization Party' but in reality fostered and promoted, it seems, by the secret 'Young Arab' group. It maintained the necessity for internal reforms giving greater freedom to both the Arabs and the other nationalities such as the Armenians, the use of Arabic as an official language, the choice of Arab officials for Arab lands, the limitation of Arab military service to their own lands, and so on. These were the maximum possible demands short of secession and the Young Turk government, concerned with the international repercussions of this Congress, tried to come to an understanding with it. This was sanctioned by a decree of the Sultan in the same year which conceded or promised almost everything that the Congress had demanded—the more so as similar claims had been put forward in the meantime by a 'Central Committee for Reform for the Defence of Syrian Rights'.

This was the culmination of the brief Arabo-Turkish idyll, timidly begun in the 1908 revolution. But even before the First World War ushered in the final crisis in Turco-Arab relations these hopes and promises had been cast away. On the Arab side, intransigent attitudes crystallized at the very moment of these concessions, disowning the collaborationist President of the Congress, Abdul Hamid al-Zahrawi, who had agreed to sit in the Ottoman senate. On the Turkish side, after experimenting with the carrot, they inevitably passed on to using the stick.

In reality the Young Turks, having come to power by their

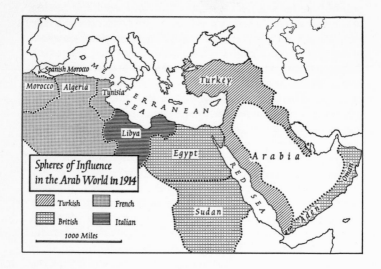

Spheres of Influence
in the Arab World in 1914

Turkish · French
British · Italian

1000 Miles

bloodless revolution, lacked true liberal feelings and cared for
the liberty of others much less than for their own. Under the
veneer of democracy, they were possessed of an intolerant
dogmatism derived from their Westernized education which
was of the illuministic radical-masonic type. This outlook had
hitherto fed the fires of Turkish nationalism and later burst into
flame with Kemalism. (At the time of which we are speaking
Mustafa Kemal himself was just making his name among the
Young Turks.) They did not, therefore, feel themselves
disposed to become the liquidators of the Ottoman Empire;
they aimed rather at patching it up and modernizing it,
reserving to the Turks their position of leadership over the
subject races. They fought hard in Libya and in the Balkan
Wars against any splitting up of the Empire, and their logical
reaction to the growing demands of Arab nationalism was
repression. In January 1914 a series of measures annulled in
practice all the concessions just granted or promised in the

political administrative fields. The dissolution of all Arab political parties was decided upon, and the forced Turcization of the non-Turkish elements of the Empire concentrated in the hands of Jemal Pasha, one of the most energetic and competent of the Young Turk leaders. What forms the struggle between Arabs and Turks might have assumed if world peace had lasted is difficult to say; certainly the unexpected crisis of the summer of 1914 and the intervention of the Turkish Empire on the side of Germany and Austria carried this conflict into a new phase, and associated the Arab cause (or at least the cause of those Arabs who were Ottoman subjects) with the whole problem of national self-determination that the war was supposed to resolve by the overthrow of the supranational empires.

The very difficult conditions in which the Syrian patriots worked, at first clandestinely under a watchful tyranny and later in the precarious liberty of the Young Turk régime, did not allow any large political movement to arise, nor any personality to become outstanding. In Egypt it was otherwise. During the same period political life developed with greater liberty, and the open activity of the parties allowed some representative figures of the Arab revival to gain stature.

The first Egyptian political party, inaugurated in 1878, was the 'Liberal Nationalist Party', with Mohammed Abduh, the disciple of Jamal al-Din al-Afghani, as its leader, around whom gathered civilians such as Abdullah al-Nadim and the young Saad Zaghlul, the future post-war leader, and soldiers such as Sami al-Barudi and Arabi Pasha. The party programme was clear from its name; it advocated resistance to intervention from abroad, a Constitution and an effective parliamentary régime at home. Therefore, even before it came into conflict with the British, it had come into conflict with the Khedives themselves, the progressive but authoritarian Ismail, and then his son and successor, Tewfik.

The anti-foreign riots of 1882, which gave Britain such a good excuse for armed intervention in Egypt, were the culmination of an internal crisis which had been brewing for some time and which brought the most dynamic representatives of the liberal nationalist movement (in particular al-Barudi and Arabi, who prevailed over the more moderate elements in the party, such as Mohammed Abduh himself) into opposition to the Khedival authority. One of the first acts the Barudi-Arabi government imposed on the Khedive in February 1882 was the dissolution of the powerless Consultative Assembly and the promulgation of a considerably wider electoral law. But British intervention (perhaps not unhappily for the Khedive), led to the trial and exile of the nationalist leaders, and marked the end of the party. The first real attempt to introduce true parliamentary life in Egypt[1] had been suffocated at birth. Some years later al-Barudi and Arabi were able to return to Egypt but not to politics. Mohammed Abduh also experienced prison and exile, but on his return maintained his moderate views, moving ever farther away from the revolutionary extremism of his master Gamal al-Din (who was not implicated in the movements of 1882, having been expelled from Egypt at the end of 1879 under British and French pressure).[2] In his later years he was one of the leaders of the 'Party of the Nation' (*Hizb al-Umma*), being fundamentally liberal and pacific, opposed to extremism and inclined to gradual reform.

The extreme nationalist programme which Arabi and the other leaders had tried to carry out in 1882, was continued by a man who can be considered the real founder of Egyptian nationalism, Mustafa Kamil (1874–1908). He was the most impassioned spokesman of Egyptian resistance in the first period of British occupation, the most resolute defender of the principle of national sovereignty, the indefatigable apostle and forerunner of independence. He had completed his education in France, at a time of intense Anglo-French rivalry. There he absorbed the culture and political ideas of the French Left (he had a long and friendly correspondence with Juliette Adam),

[1] From 1883 to 1912, Egypt had two representative bodies, the 'Legislative Council' and the 'General Assembly', neither more than consultative.

[2] He passed his last years in Constantinople where he died in 1897, as the guest, or rather the prisoner, of Abdul Hamid, who had persuaded him to share his unrealistic schemes for pan-Islamism.

and perhaps nursed the hope of French aid to rid his country of British domination. The Anglo-French agreement of 1904, which allowed Great Britain a free hand in Egypt, blasted these hopes, but did not entirely destroy his sympathy with France, the mother of liberty.

The political programme of Mustafa Kamil, expressed in his impassioned oratory and in his paper *al-Liwa* (*The Standard*, founded in 1900) amd later in his party, which was called simply the 'National Party' (*a-Hizb al-Watani*), officially formed in 1907, had features which in the light of later events must already have seemed old fashioned, such as the reaffirmation of the supreme sovereignty of the Ottoman government over Egypt. But the cardinal points of his programme were the ending of foreign occupation and intervention, and the institution of constitutional government, in substance the same principles for which the men of 1882 had fought and lost. The recognition of the formal link with Constantinople (which was nominally maintained till 1914) was partly a stick to beat the British with and partly homage to the ideal, much discussed at that time, of pan-Islamism within the terms of which, following the doctrine of Gamal al-Din, Mustafa Kamil believed an Egyptian national revival had its place. Furthermore, to achieve the complete independence of the country he wanted to unite all his countrymen, whether Moslem or Copt; and although firm in demanding the withdrawal of all foreign forces from the Nile Valley, he stressed the need for concord and friendship between Egyptians and foreigners and for cordial relations with the nations of Europe.

The nationalism of Mustafa Kamil had nothing of that narrow hatred of foreigners that was to mark other and later phases of Arab and Oriental nationalism. His motto, 'free in our own country, and generous to our guests', claimed liberty for his country as the inalienable right of every people, while holding out his hand to other peoples in peaceful competition for civil and cultural progress.[1] He acknowledged Egypt's duty

[1] Kamil worked enthusiastically for the improvement of education in Egypt, and proposed a national university.

to respect her treaties with and financial obligations to European powers and was even willing to allow outside financial control, which should, however, be sanctioned by all the powers and not left to the absolute discretion of only one of them. With Kamil's intransigence on Egyptian independence were coupled principles that would today be considered moderate. Even if due in part to tactical reasons, they corresponded to his own noble spirit and to the ideals of the general liberty and brotherhood of peoples he had absorbed from his European education.

In the name of those ideals Mustafa Kamil in 1896 turned to Gladstone, under whose government the intervention of 1882 had taken place, calling on him to give his views on the legality of a British occupation of Egypt indefinitely prolonged, and the old statesman, who had at one time raised his voice in favour of Italian liberty, responded loyally, expressing his view that England should henceforth put an end to an occupation considered by him at least to be temporary, and which was no longer justified by the circumstances that had provoked it. But the Britain of those years, the Britain of Chamberlain and Kitchener, was certainly not the country to listen to that lonely voice.

Surprising as it may seem in the mid-twentieth century, Mustafa Kamil's activities went on in broad daylight, in full liberty and legality. However little favoured by the High Commissioner, he was none the less neither greatly hindered nor persecuted. 'The English', Mustafa Kamil wrote to Mlle Adam in 1906 when France wanted to forbid the distribution of his paper in Tunisia as anti-British, 'leave me full freedom of action here, subscribe to my paper and grant me a leading part in official ceremonies. . . .'

When the Dinshawi incident of 1906 (a village affray, involving some British officers after which death sentences and long terms of hard labour were passed on their *fellah* attackers) inflamed Egyptian public opinion against the occupiers, Mustafa Kamil was able to express his disgust at the unreasonable scale of the punishments in his own paper and in papers abroad without being molested. Needless to say he was constantly attacked by the collaborationists in Egyptian society and by the Egyptian Press. These attacks ended by his falling out with the Khedive himself. He always had persistent rivals and detractors, but the younger Egyptian generation saw him as their leader, and rallied to him in his struggle. He died in 1908 when he was scarcely thirty-four. A just historical judgement must call him the precursor of the political resurrection of modern Egypt, and acknowledge in him those traits of chivalry, generosity and idealism which seem to have been, both in the East and in the West, the best heritage of the nineteenth century.

The 'National Party' which Mustafa Kamil had brought into being did not survive for long, once deprived of the remarkable personality of its founder. Rent by internal dissensions it was dissolved in 1912 after the discovery of a nationalist plot against the Khedive and Kitchener. The rival 'Party of the Nation' of more moderate views, led by Mohammed Abduh, had a slightly longer life, up to 1914. But the ideas of both parties were revived in Egyptian political life after the war. The moderates regrouped themselves in 1922 in the party of the Liberal Constitutionalists, while the intransigent nationalist wing, which was backed by the great majority of the Egyptian people, was represented by the *Wafd* under Zaghlul. He had not fought with Kamil's party in his youth and had actually come from the ranks of the 'Party of the Nation', but he assumed the heritage of the young nationalist leader and carried it on towards victory in the recent history of Egypt. Mustafa Kamil and Saad Zaghlul were the last leaders of Arab-Egyptian nationalism in whom it was still possible to recognize traces of Mazzini and Garibaldi. Their successors belong entirely to the new century and speak a different language.

Early Arab nationalism in Syria and Egypt (and elsewhere) is often accused of completely ignoring social problems. Representing the *élite* of the cities and the middle classes, with the support of the great landlords, it concentrated exclusively on questions of national autonomy and independence and representative institutions, without appearing to be aware of the grave economic inequalities and social injustices that had for centuries afflicted the Arab peoples and all the peoples of the East.[1] In this the Arab revival was, generally speaking, evolving along the same lines as nationalist revivals in Europe. These too were led by the *bourgeois élite*, conservative on the whole in social affairs, until, the political revival having worked itself out, the proletariat made its appearance on the scene, marking a separate phase in the evolution of nations. Only nowadays does the progress of the Arab revival give signs of recognizing the weight and urgency of social problems. We shall come back to these later in the contemporary history of the Arab world, but the remark in all its negative implications holds good for the dawning of the national movement with which we are now dealing.

While the first germs of the revival were thus fermenting in the Fertile Crescent and in Egypt, the Arab West, the Maghreb, finally fell under complete European control in the early 1900s. The Italian occupation of Libya wiped out the last vestige of Turkish dominion in North Africa, notwithstanding Italy's equivocal recognition of a so-called 'spiritual sovereignty' of the Caliph at Constantinople over the area. The Turks had in fact put up a fight to preserve this borderland of their decaying Empire, and the local Arabs had stood by them in a sense of community of faith and out of an instinctive aversion to the foreign invader.

Resistance was broken more easily in Tripolitania than in Cyrenaica, where the powerful Senussi brotherhood had established a *de facto* state under nominal Turkish rule. The Senussi were the main instigators of resistance and revolt, though more in the name of the pure Islamic tradition than from any feeling of a modern national consciousness.

In the farthest west, Morocco, the sole Arab country untouched by Ottoman hegemony, opened at last to European influences and, finally, to two European protectorates. The

[1] A notable exception, at this time, was Qasim Amin's campaign for the emancipation of women, already mentioned.

Sheriffian Empire which had been able to sustain its independence from the sixteenth to the nineteenth century against Portuguese, Spaniards and Turks, lost it in 1912 after years of political skirmishing among the European powers. It accepted the Protectorate of France over all the rest of its territory, even as it had earlier submitted to that of Spain over the north-western coastal area. This was made possible by the state of anarchy into which the country had fallen, due to the continual rebellions of the tribes of the interior against the authority of the Sultan, which the French set out to restore in their own way and to their own advantage. The ability and humanity of Lyautey still shine forth in this military, political and civil achievement. He was able to impose French colonial authority with the least possible force and with the maximum respect for local traditions, creating a model administration, which greatly benefited the material progress and the culture of Morocco. But history was to prove this work more ephemeral than it seemed at the time, turning its virtues back upon their promoters.

Thus in the early years of the century, the Arab world felt at one and the same time the first symptoms of political reawakening and the completion of its subjugation to foreign peoples and states. The First World War came to sharpen this antithesis.

World War I and its Aftermath

World War I and its Aftermath

THE WAR OF 1914–18 might be called the beginning of the political suicide of Europe in the eyes of the whole Oriental world. The Eastern peoples saw the West, which had until then weighed upon them with all of its formidable technical and moral authority, divide into rival camps and tear itself to pieces.

The Arabs were fully involved in this struggle, and naturally hoped to take advantage of it in recovering their lost liberty. Faced with the choice between pan-Islamic solidarity, which the Ottoman Empire tried to invoke when it entered the war on the side of the Central Powers, and the promises of liberty and national independence and of respect for and aid to the will of the various oppressed peoples held out by the *Entente*, the Arabs of the East elected almost unanimously for the latter, in accordance with their long-standing desire to free themselves from Ottoman rule. To have broken these promises, in the spirit and also partly in the letter, was a grave error of the victors after the First World War, and sowed the seeds of delusion and a burning rancour still not entirely extinct in the Arab world.

In spite of this · partial unfulfilment and their perhaps exaggerated sense of disillusion, the Arabs made their first decisive steps towards full national liberation both during the conflict and in the reorganization that followed it. The Arabs of the West remained, meanwhile, as a whole loyal to their European tutors and colonizers and spent their tribute of blood and gave every support for what then seemed a common cause no less than the Arabs of the East. At the same time they were maturing a sharper national consciousness and with it demands for political rights, which were later on to stimulate their struggle for freedom.

Thus from Mesopotamia to Morocco the cause of the Central Powers, where it existed, rested on military force alone; while the work of their diplomats and their secret agents achieved the minimum result,[1] since they were unable to appeal to the ideal of independence of the Arab peoples when that very ideal was being trampled upon in the Arab homelands by their Turkish ally.

The Arab countries which suffered the most during the First World War were those of the Fertile Crescent, which were subjected to a harsh Turco-German military rule leading to a very severe economic crisis and food shortage, with consequent famines, epidemics and every sort of privation. The Arab lands became an important sphere of military operations on the international and imperial plane of the great conflict.

Syria, which had been the centre of the Arab movements for autonomy or separatism, was suddenly made helpless by the pitiless energy of Jemal Pasha, who took over the defence of the threatened Empire with dictatorial powers. In 1915 and 1916, while the Turks and Germans were launching repeated and fruitless attacks on the Suez Canal, the courts martial of Jemal in Damascus and Beirut sent to the gallows scores of Arab patriots accused (often with good reason) of anti-Turkish plots and connivance with the enemy, revealed by compromising records found in the French consulates. Amongst those first martyrs who went to their death were the former President of the Paris Congress, Abdul Hamid al-Zahrawi, Omar al-Jazairi nephew of the heroic Abdul-Kader, journalists and magistrates, Moslems and Christians, whilst other death sentences *in contumaciam* struck at Syrians and Lebanese resident in Egypt.

Thus something similar to the drama of the Austro-Hungarian Empire, compelled to defend itself by drastic measures against its own rebellious satellites, was repeated in the East; and a just historical judgement, in the East as well as in the West, cannot deny the legal right of the persecutors, whilst acknowledging the higher right and the halo of matyrdom for their victims. That all these fell for the ideal of Arab liberty is beyond doubt, even if the method by which they wished to see its realization was rather more narrowly Syrian or Lebanese than pan-Arab;

[1] The one exception was Libya, where the Turks and Germans succeeded in making almost the whole country rise in revolt, restricting the Italian occupation to the coastal centres.

not complete independence but some sort of dependence on, and association with, the protection of France. This last was an idea repugnant to later extreme nationalist movements, but at that time it must have been favoured at least by certain Christians of the Lebanon. Though fruitful in the long run, as is every martyrdom, the Syrian holocaust seemed for the moment useless, since the country remained paralysed by Ottoman martial law, but the leadership of the Arab revolt was taken over by others in other more distant countries and in more propitious conditions.

In the Arabian Peninsula, once the cradle of the Arab peoples and of the Moslem faith, there were two kinds of authority; Turkish rule, which had installed itself there in the sixteenth century, and the local authority of dynasties and chiefs of various states and principalities, amongst whom the Sherif of Mecca was pre-eminent. Descended from a Mecca family to which the Prophet himself had belonged (hence the title of Sherif and the epithet Hashemite, that is to say of the race of Hashim of which Mohammed himself was a member) this Emir exercised a power transmitted hereditarily since the thirteenth century, though subject to supreme Ottoman sovereignty.

The Emir at that time, Husein, had not remained unmoved by the current of revolt that was stirring the Arab world, and his sons, Feisal and Abdullah, had both been associated with various pan-Arab irredentist Associations and Leagues. In 1915, while the Turks were impatiently demanding his active participation in the Holy War recently proclaimed, Husein began to make cautious contact with the Allies, to sound their views in the event of an Arab revolt. To brand this as a double game, as certain adversaries of the Arab claims have done, is to ignore the extreme delicacy of Husein's position. He found himself negotiating with Britain about the political promises of the *Entente* while Turkish garrisons were in his own land and his son Feisal was in Syria as a hostage.

However, the negotiations with Britain, through the High Commissioner in Egypt, MacMahon, went on between July

1915 and March 1916 (we shall shortly examine the agreements then discussed), and led to a complete understanding, or at least one that was so regarded by Husein. In June 1916, having obtained the return of Feisal from Syria, the Sherif of Mecca proclaimed the Arab revolt on the side of the Allies and rapidly made himself master of almost all the Hejaz, save for Medina where the Turkish garrison sustained a long siege. Thenceforward the final task of the Hashemite forces commanded by Feisal was to press forward from the desert on to the left flank of the Turco-German battle-line, which stretched in Palestine from Gaza to Beersheba, and to help break it up.

This was the famous two-year guerrilla campaign in the desert, immortalized by T. E. Lawrence; and this was the sole front on which the Arabs fought as an autonomous unit (the Iraqi tribes had remained inactive, British plans for an insurrection there having failed owing to the opposition of the Indian Government, and the campaign there was waged exclusively with Anglo-Indian forces). Under the command of Feisal, assisted by Lawrence and an Iraqi-Arab officer, Jafar al-Askari, some of the Hejaz tribes and the Transjordan tribes of the Huweitat and Ruwala with their respective chiefs, Auda Abu Tai and Nuri Shaalan, fought in the Syrian-Arabian desert. They are well known to readers of Lawrence's *Revolt in the Desert* and *The Seven Pillars of Wisdom*, the historical and imaginative commentary on this war.

Judgements of its conduct and value have varied from those who see in it the valid justification for the independence of the Arabs, the invaluable and later defrauded allies of the *Entente* in the East, to those on the other hand who decry this support, considering it no more than a slight and inconclusive factor in the campaign carried out in Palestine and Syria by the Anglo-French forces. The truth seems to lie half-way between these extremes; the action of the bedouin was, it is true, more of nuisance value than anything else, carried out as it was with very limited resources and on a scale to be expected from desert nomads. But that does not invalidate the courage and individual sacrifice which, according to the testimony of Lawrence and also of other more impartial observers, were not lacking in such conditions, nor does it diminish the weight of Turco-German arms that this guerrilla warfare was able to distract and hold down in Syria.

It should also be borne in mind that the anti-Sherif and anti-Hejaz polemists insist on decrying this bedouin aid by stressing the contribution that the Arabs elsewhere—in Egypt, Syria and the other Arab lands at that time under Ottoman rule—made to the war in units commanded by the Allies. They thereby recognize the fact that the Arab did really make sacrifices for a common cause. But on the other hand the idea of a common Arab revolt then appeared to certain Western observers as so absurd that they put the Hejaz Arabs on the same level as those of the other lands of the Fertile Crescent, as people trying vainly to realize the great pan-Arab dream which had possessed the Sherif of Mecca, Husein.[1]

Let us briefly recall the broad outlines of the Anglo-Franco-Arab campaigns of 1917–18, which brought four centuries of Turkish rule in the Fertile Crescent to an end. In the spring of 1917, the British forces in Palestine led by Allenby began to bear against the strongly-prepared Gaza-Beersheba line, defended by the German and Turkish troops under von Falkenhayn's command. A decisive victory did not come to the Allies until November, with the taking of Gaza and Jaffa, and in the first days of December, with the entry into Jerusalem. In the meantime Feisal and Lawrence's Arabs were advancing along the west coast of the Peninsula and in July of the same year they occupied Aqaba. From there they invaded Transjordan. By repeated surprise attacks, their guerrilla units were especially effective in disrupting the Hejaz railway line which was vital to the Turks and Germans for bringing up reinforcements to the front. The great Transjordanian tribe, the Huwaitat, distinguished itself in the final capture of the

[1] This anti-Hashemite and, in final analysis, anti-Arab viewpoint was one that inspired the *Précis Historique* on Syria by Lammens (Beirut 1921) a great Orientalist but not a calm historian of these events, which he judged with a spirit of French chauvinism.

historic railroad which had been inaugurated only a few years before the war.

Not surprisingly, the lightly armed and inexperienced desert forces met with less success in their attacks against strongly fortified and well-defended centres such as Maan.

In the winter of 1917–18 the main Palestine front stabilized itself on a line stretching from the north of Jaffa to Jericho in Jordan. The decisive operations which Allenby planned for the summer of 1918 were based on a break-through on the front in the plains of Sarona, while the Arabs interrupted work on the Hejaz railway north of Deraa, which would cut the line of communication between Damascus and Transjordan. The latter task was brilliantly carried out by Lawrence and the Iraqi colonel Nuri Bey (the future Nuri al-Said Pasha, for many years virtual dictator of Iraq). At the same time the successful breaching of the Turco-German front at Sarona (end of September 1918) completed the liberation of Palestine. General Liman von Sanders, who had succeeded Falkenhayn, still tried in vain to defend southern Syria, first from the Tiberias line, then from Rayaq, but the distintegration of his forces made this impossible. The most coveted fruit of victory, Damascus was taken on 1st October, 1918 by Feisal, Lawrence and their men, who entered it in triumph. The victory owed as much to Arab sacrifices, from the Syrian martyrs of 1915–16 to all the bedouin fallen in Arabia and Transjordan in the two-year war and all the Arabs who had fought bravely in the Allied ranks, as to the Allied forces. For the young Hashemite prince who on that day entered the Syrian capital, as his ancestors had done in the great days of the Islamic conquests, there could be no doubt that if he believed the promises and agreements that had been made to him, the military victory marked the beginning of a great and free Arab state.

But what precisely had been those promises and those agreements? The key of the dispute on this point, which dragged on for the whole of the twenty years between the two wars amid bitter recriminations and hypocritical quibbles, was the correspondence exchanged in 1915 and 1916 between the

British High Commissioner in Cairo, MacMahon, and the Sherif of Mecca, Husein (published in full in 1938 and in the official English version in 1939). From these letters Husein appeared to believe that he had reached a precise understanding with Great Britain on the formation of a unified Arab state comprising the whole zone of the Fertile Crescent and the Arabian Peninsula, that is in all the Arab lands of the dissolving Ottoman Empire. His original demands were even wider: he wanted to include such areas of somewhat doubtful 'Arabness' as the Turkish provinces of Mersin and Adana, but MacMahon induced him to drop this idea. He also made special conditions with regard to the coastal zone of Syria (that is, the Lebanon) as being of particular interest to France, and on Iraq (provinces of Baghdad and Basrah) where British interests were involved; while rejecting all Anglo-French claims in principle, Husein consented to discuss these conditions later.

Not a word on the other hand was said about Palestine, overlooked either deliberately or accidentally in the British observations; and although twenty years later MacMahon in a letter to *The Times* declared candidly that he had not even thought at that time of including it in the promised lands, logic and geography fully authorized the Arabs to consider it a part of their territory 'bounded on the West by the Red Sea and the Mediterranean as far as Mersin', as their demands were set forth.

Even apart from Palestine, it cannot honestly be denied that from that very first moment Great Britain had made some reservations on the maximum programme of the Arab nationalists (Husein's demands had reiterated almost word for word those of the Syrian irredentists that had been passed on to him in secret meetings in Damascus) both as regards French interests in Lebanon-Syria and British interests in Iraq. But what had been merely outlined in the correspondence with Husein as a possible subject for later discussion, was developed and precisely specified in a crudely imperialist spirit in successive secret Franco-British documents.

These were the ill-famed Sykes-Picot agreements of May 1916 (the ink was scarcely dry on the correspondence between

Cairo and Mecca), made known in November 1917 by the Russian Bolsheviks, which amounted to a somewhat cynical partition of the Arab lands of the Ottoman Empire according to exclusively Anglo-French interests. These provided for a western zone of the Fertile Crescent (Lebanon and the coastline of Syria) generously rounded off by Cilicia and other parts of Turkey, and another, eastern, zone including the larger and better part of Iraq. In these zones France and England respectively 'seront autoriseés à établir telle administration directe ou indirecte ou tel contrôle qu'elles désirent . . .', all Palestine (save for the ports of Acre and Haifa reserved to Britain) was internationalized and, as an act of kindness, an inner Arab state (which might well be called 'The Desert State') was in its turn to be divided into two zones of French and English influence respectively!

The Sykes-Picot agreements therefore transformed the vague reservations of MacMahon on the great Arab state into a ruthless amputation from it of almost all the fertile lands of the Crescent (Palestine this time explicitly included). They restricted that state to the Syrian-Arabian desert, depriving it of any sort of outlet to the sea, although leaving it on the east Mosul and on the west the cities of inner Syria with Damascus, a fine consolation, had they but known, for the Arab patriots who at that very time were being hanged there! Whether Grey with his French colleague, Cambon (Sykes and Picot were only the direct negotiators), remembered or overlooked that a few months before he had been treating through MacMahon with the Sherif Husein, is a matter for speculation. When Husein was informed by the Turks of the Sykes-Picot documents published by the Bolsheviks, he asked the British Government for an explanation and received general reassurances on the irrevocable intention of the Allies to support to the utmost the cause of all oppressed peoples and of the Arabs in particular though all in rather vague terms. In the meantime another act of the British Government with consequences for the future of Palestine was being drawn up: the Balfour Declaration of November 1917 on the Jewish National Home in that land

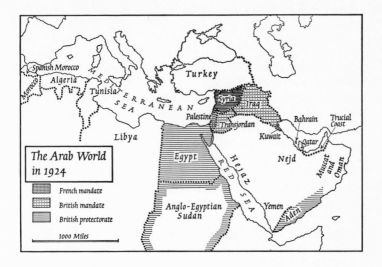

The Arab World
in 1924

French mandate
British mandate
British protectorate

1000 Miles

Spanish Morocco
Morocco
Algeria
Tunisia
MEDITERRANEAN SEA
Turkey
Syria
Iraq
Palestine
Transjordan
Bahrain
Trucial Coast
Kuwait
Qatar
Libya
Egypt
Hejaz
RED SEA
Nejd
Muscat and Oman
Anglo-Egyptian Sudan
Yemen
Aden

where the hopes and aims of Zionism had been fixed ever since the times of Herzl and Abdul Hamid.

Relations between Arabs and Jews in the next two decades have been so disastrous that it is worth while recalling one act of good will or of good policy between the representatives of the two peoples at a time when the war was scarcely over. This was the Weizmann-Feisal agreement of 6th January, 1919, when the greatest spokesman of Arab interests and the leader of Zionism 'recalling the racial affinity and the bonds existing of old between the Arab and Hebrew peoples, and considering that the surest means for the attainment of their national aspirations consist of the closest possible collaboration in the development of an Arab state and of Palestine' (words which today it seems impossible could ever have been exchanged between an Arab and a Jew!), agreed to negotiate every dispute between them, beginning with that of frontiers, in a spirit of concord and good will. But a marginal note by Feisal, who was

73

certainly in the right here, makes this agreement conditional upon the granting of Arab independence according to his well-known maximum demands; and the downfall of these Arab expectations also destroyed all hopes of peaceful Arab-Jewish relations. This was the most difficult of the problems that the First World War left as a legacy to those who followed, and it still remains unsolved today.

These were in fact the political actions and obligations, open or secret, defined or undefined that should have been on the conference table for the solution of the Arab problem. In reality these individual obligations, some of which had already been disowned, were heavily outweighed by the self-interest of France and Britain. America had neither the power nor the wish to oppose her Allies, merely to grant some satisfaction to Arab irredentism and nationalism. The British interests required a firm control of Iraq, a strong region of great strategic importance, since it lay on the route to India, and also since it contained the Mosul oilfields—a source of wealth awaiting exploitation as the Persian oilfields had already been exploited.

The French, on the other hand, were more concerned with realizing their centuries-old mission of faith, civilization and culture in Syria and the Lebanon. Both powers felt they had a duty and a right to intervene in the delicate and complicated problems of the Holy Places which the Balfour Declaration, the Magna Charta of Zionism, had recently complicated still more. Not all these interests and motives, therefore, were merely material and self-seeking, and all of them could be justified by confidence, unshaken in Europe for forty years, of the superiority and maturity of the West when compared with the young and restless Oriental peoples who until yesterday were simple subjects of an archaic Empire in dissolution, but who now aspired to an autonomous political life. The need for long and gradual training in self-government, for economic and technical aid, for safeguarding the European colonies in the Levant, were all more or less sincere arguments that made the European victors of the First World War oppose the total and complete independence of the Arabs, and see themselves as teachers and tutors of the Arabs' obvious immaturity.

Thus was born, in the Wilsonian-imperialist climate of victory (if one can link, as one has to, a high and Utopian idealism with a conception and a practice far less idealist) the international institution of the Mandate, which aimed at reconciling the principle of self-determination of peoples with their gradual education for liberty; a process to which it is difficult to set limits since the end of the teaching must coincide with the withdrawal of the teachers and the end of all the privileges and advantages accruing from their duties.

The application of the 'mandate' solution for the Arab peoples of the dismembered Ottoman Empire was gradually extended through 1919 and 1920, amid the exasperated disillusion of those who had cherished the dream of a great Arab state, free and united, even if subject to limitations. Unity was the first of the ideals that had to be given up. This was not merely a dynastic ambition of Husein (who proclaimed himself in 1916 as King of the Arabs but was prudently recognized by the Allies only as King of the Hejaz), but was also in keeping with their common origin, language and most glorious traditions. The principle of *divide et impera* led the powers to encourage every local difference that might lead to divisions of the Crescent into individual states.

The Arabian Peninsula that should have been the nucleus of the new state, as it had been of the ancient empire, was abandoned to its own resources. In Syria, martyr of the early days of the revival, Feisal had been welcomed in 1918 as a liberator, and the dream of a Syrian kingdom was cherished by the Hashemite prince up to 1920; but while in March of that year he had proclaimed himself King of Syria, the San Remo Conference in April sanctioned the principle of mandates, assigning Syria and Lebanon to France and Mesopotamia and Palestine to Britain. The brief and equivocal Franco-Hashemite condominium in Syria lasted only a few months. It ended by force when the artillery of General Gouraud scattered the hastily gathered troops of Feisal near Damascus (July 1920). Thus he

75

had to leave for ever that promised land which he had helped to liberate and for which, as for the rest of the Arab world, he had demanded complete independence before the Great Powers at the Paris Conference.

The mandatory system was completed between 1922 and 1924 by solemn enactments of the League of Nations. Instead of the hoped-for united Arab state, the Arabs of the former Ottoman Empire found themselves divided into a constellation of regional states, partly monarchial (Iraq and Transjordan), partly republican (Lebanon and Syria) and one without any definite political character (Palestine), but all controlled by British or French Commissioners. For each one of them a separate history began, though they all shared a common disillusion and bitterness at the injustice committed against the programme of national unity and independence. This bitterness and disillusion did not prevent them from building themselves up as nations in the limited form to which they were now reduced. When the Second World War broke out, they were far better placed than they had been at the outbreak of the First; but the way this partition was carried out contributed, as we shall see, to the series of political and civic crises that beset the whole Arab world during those twenty years, and to the new phase of Arab extremist nationalism, that marks the period closest to us.

In these transactions, Great Britain at least deserves credit not due to France for her genuine, if tardy, qualm of conscience over Palestine and for the fact that reservations were made in the first agreement, vague though they were. But her opposition to the Egyptian liberation movement, which exploded in the first years after the war with unexpected violence, was frankly imperialist. The 'temporary' military occupation set up in 1882 revealed itself openly in December 1914 by the deposition of the Khedive, Abbas Hilmi, who was considered to be in sympathy with Turkey and Germany, and the proclamation of the British Protectorate over Egypt. The country bowed its head without resistance, with a genuine sense of being protected, although it had been just a part of British imperial interests, during the First World War. But as soon as this was over, when the Wilsonian principles of self-determination were everywhere being discussed, Egypt again leapt to her feet to demand the independence it failed to gain thirty-five years before.

The leader of this struggle in its first and most dramatic phases, and a true 'father of his country' was Saad Zaghlul (1860–1927), the son of peasants from the Nile Valley, of unshaken Mazzinian faith in the justice of his cause, and indefatigably tenacious in achieving it. He too in his youth had been a disciple of Gamal al-Din al-Afghani and friend of Mohammed Abduh and belonged to the Arabi movement, but later he preferred to range himself with the moderates of the first decade of the century, so much so as to win the good will of Lord Cromer.[1] But in the first years after the war he returned to the policies of Mustafa Kamil and reaffirmed Egypt's right to full independence and the withdrawal of the occupying forces.[2]

A group of Egyptian leaders with Zaghlul at their head formed themselves into a *Wafd* or delegation to the forthcoming Peace Conference. Two days after the Armistice in Europe, he had placed their demands before an astounded British High Commissioner. The British reply was a prohibition to the *Wafd* to go to Paris and, at the outbreak of the first bazaar riots, the arrest of Zaghlul with three other nationalist leaders and their deportation to Malta (March 1919). But the riots grew worse and Allenby, the victor of the war in the East and now appointed High Commissioner in Egypt, was obliged to try a policy of conciliation. He set free the exiles and allowed Zaghlul to go to Paris.

The Milner mission (December 1919—March 1920), tried to find a compromise with Egyptian aspirations, which in the meantime had received from Wilson a far from edifying *fin de non recevoir* at the Paris Conference, and there were further

[1] With Cromer's support Zaghlul was given the Ministry of Education in 1907.
[2] Only the unilateral British Proclamation of the Protectorate in 1914 and the Treaty of Sèvres in 1920 recalled to the world at large that vestige of the Turkish sovereignty over Egypt, that formal link about which so many Egyptians, including the nationalist Mustafa Kamil had shown themselves sensitive.

77

unfruitful negotiations between the nationalist leaders and the London Government. In December 1921 the British returned to a policy of force, with a fresh arrest of Zaghlul and his deportation to the Seychelles, but the very violent reaction of the country once again induced them to compromise. On 28th February, 1922 Britain proclaimed the end of the Protectorate and the 'independence' of Egypt, which was at the same time rendered dependent (seemingly a paradox but reflecting the firm determination not to relinquish the prey) by four reserved points: the security of imperial communications in Egypt, defence, foreign affairs and, finally, the Sudan (under formal Anglo-Egyptian Condominium since 1899, though Kitchener's reconquest after the Madhist insurrection served British interest alone). The Sultan Fuad, a young son of Ismail, who succeeded the deposed Khedive in 1917 as nominal sovereign (after his elder but short-lived brother), assumed the title of king and on 15th March inaugurated the 'independent' Kingdom of Egypt with a continuing British occupation.

The *Wafd*, which had in the meantime transformed itself into a real political party, did not recognize the British Proclamation of 28th February because of the contradictory nature of its compromise. None the less a first and noteworthy step forward towards effective independence had been made enabling Egypt to reacquire international status, ending the purely military régime and paving the way for parliamentary life. The merit of this first success was due firstly to the courageous integrity of Zaghlul and secondly to the whole Egyptian people, who had supported him in those years of struggle with marvellous unanimity: Moslems and Copts, men and women, pashas, students and peasants all standing together. The *Wafd* had absorbed every other political group and so left no more moderate force with which Britain could balance its enormous popularity. It was only in 1922 with the promulgation the following year of the first constitution and a parliamentary system on the European model, that a party struggle began in Egypt. Egyptian internal politics were for thirty years a three-cornered struggle between Britain, the Crown and the political parties. The outstanding phases of this struggle will follow later.

Britain therefore (seconded by France, but only for the ex-Ottoman Levant) did all she could to oppose the drive for Arab independence in that first post-war period; a drive which was continued by the Arabs, separately, there being only a vague solidarity of ideal between the struggle in Egypt (which at that time showed very little interest in the pan-Arab movement) and that of the various regions of the Fertile Crescent, divided and subdivided by the self-appointed administrators. The great dream of an Arab unity faded, and each part of the Arab world withdrew into itself, concerned with its own problems and interests, rather than with the problem of freeing itself from new or old masters.

It would, however, be unjust to ignore the positive character of the change from the hegemony of a decadent and decaying Oriental Empire to the technically efficient and often intelligent and far-seeing guardianship of two great modern nations. France and Britain had already given the East the best of their thought, their culture and their technical efficiency, and continued to pour them out, helping these backward satellites of the Ottoman Empire to make great steps forward on the road to progress. But these undeniable advantages were vitiated by the mandatory régime that had been imposed upon the peoples, who in the best European traditions of the nineteenth century had always placed liberty and national independence at the summit of their ideals. A tension was created, which explains a great deal of Arab history in the twenty years between the wars —a tension even further complicated by the crisis of ideals in Europe itself.

To sum up: the partition invented and imposed by Europe on the peoples in the first years after the war was lacking in trust, fairness and faith; and even if these qualities alone cannot regulate relations between peoples and states, the experience of the Arab peoples shows that to ignore them totally only defeats the very purposes of *Realpolitik*.

The Arab States between the Wars

The Arab States between the Wars

DESPITE THE SUFFERINGS, sacrifices and disillusions, the First World War had given the Arabs a chance to make a considerable step towards the realization of their aims. The Fertile Crescent now consisted not of neglected Ottoman *vilayets* but of a group of states whose right to independence, even if limited in practice by the tutelary mandates, had been recognized. Egypt too at the end of the war had found a fresh incentive to enter fully into the struggle for national independence. Notwithstanding the apparent revival of imperialism in Europe just after the war, in sharp contrast to the principles then publicly affirmed, facts showed that it was impossible to turn back and that the ambiguous structure of the mandates, imperfectly concealing the old aims of domination and exploitation, was sooner or later bound to collapse even as in Egypt the anachronistic attempt of Great Britain to cling to politico-military control of the Nile Valley was also bound to collapse.

The struggle between teachers and taught, between the protectors and their unruly wards eager to shake off every form of protection and tutelage, was to fill the whole interval of twenty years between the two world conflagrations, and was not to be ended until long after the end of the second. In that struggle the Arabs consumed all their energies and subordinated every other problem, whether economic or social, to the *primum necessarium* of effective independence. It is therefore not surprising that civil education should have achieved so little and that the question of the liberty of the individual should hardly have been touched upon.

Relations with the occupiers in Egypt and with the 'mandatory power' in the countries of the Crescent conditioned every programme and every political activity, from intransigent nationalism to temporizing collaboration and open support and service of the foreigner (examples of all three of these attitudes were not lacking among the Arab rulers and politicians), and this certainly did not help to make a sane and effective democratic life within the individual countries. The Arabs had had democracy dinned into their ears by wartime propaganda, and democratic institutions (parties and parliaments) were suddenly introduced into all the new states, with the exception of Transjordan and Saudi Arabia which were still somewhat backward.

But foreign policy dominated everything and everyone, and the life of parliaments and parties was carried on almost wholly in its shadow. Faith in civil liberties and democratic methods, which were closely associated with the pre-war ideal of independence, began to waver after the war, perhaps as a result of the decline of those ideals in Europe itself. Facism in Italy and then Nazism in Germany, Bolshevism in Russia and Kemalism in Turkey, all placed before the eyes of the Arabs examples of peoples rising out of disorder and defeat under the guidance of authoritarian leaders and régimes free from parliamentary scruples and restrictions, affirming the *salus populi* as the supreme law to be followed by any and every means. And what on the other hand had the Western democracies offered to the peoples of the East? Unfulfilled promises and ambiguous or open abuses of power.

The crisis of ideals which was to be seen in the whole of the Arab world in the twenty years between the two wars was therefore quite comprehensible and was nourished and encouraged in every way by at least some of the European countries mentioned above. When the representatives and spokesmen of democracy were identified with the hated 'occupiers', and the struggle was described as between 'haves' and 'have-nots', the Arabs for the most part fell into the trap, forgetting or pretending to forget that they themselves, together with all the other 'inferior' peoples, were the prizes for which the more powerful nations contended.

The injustices of Versailles and, in particular, the unedifying political settlement of the Near East, had become, well before the new conflict, one of the favourite themes of totalitarian propaganda, and it would have been too much to ask of the Arabs to realize the tendentiousness, the distortions and the exaggerations in these half-truths, and the dishonesty of those who posed as the champions of liberty abroad while at the same time reducing their own citizens to slavery. How, in fact, the Nazis and Fascists generally understood the liberty of other peoples in their power was to be seen in Libya and Ethiopia even before the Second World War and later, both inside and outside Europe, wherever German rule was briefly established.[1] In the twenty years between the two wars, in fact, the nineteenth-century ideals in which the forerunners of the Arab revival had believed were more or less openly set aside, and the concept of independence-and-liberty which had appeared inseparable was divided, only the first of these two demands was accentuated and isolated.

Even those who had no illusions about the real intentions of the Italian and German 'liberators' (and it would be to wrong the intelligence of the Arabs to think that none amongst them were aware of them) ended by accepting the claim of authoritarianism to be the most serviceable and expeditious method of government for the attainment of high aims, since after all they were the enemies of their enemies. The evil efficiency of false democracies and real dictatorships made the Arabs, in the hard struggle that was still before them, lose a great part of their original ideals. Nazism and Fascism were formative influences on the harshest and most violent phase of Arab nationalism, which began to grow in just those twenty years, even as the the liberalism and democracy of the West had been earlier.

Turkish and Soviet models also had an effect in obscuring democratic ideals among the Arabs but they were secondary; and, in both cases, for predominantly religious reasons. Kemalism and Bolshevism, especially in their earlier phases, had both shown themselves very hostile to religion (i.e. Islam); and though, in the new nationalism of the Arabs, the religious sentiment had begun to give way to the ethnic one, it still retained

---

[1] Italian repression in Libya and during the Ethiopian campaign aroused violent reactions in the Press and public opinion of the Arab lands.

enough vigour to make the Arabs hesitant and suspicious towards such examples. When the Soviet Union inaugurated a religious policy that was at least formally more tolerant these suspicions and reservations began to disappear, especially since in the changed groupings of the years after the Second World War, she ostentatiously took the part of the Eastern peoples against the relics of the old, and the aspirations of the revived imperialism.

Between the two wars another factor contributed to feed the discontent, the rancour, the restlessness and the exasperation of the Arabs; this was the Palestine problem, recklessly created by Great Britain during the First World War and handed on unsolved to the Second, and beyond. Leaving until later the basic facts and dates, we may merely observe here that this problem has irreparably compromised a sincere friendship between the Arab world and the Western bloc (if we may be allowed to anticipate the vocabulary of our own age) and provided a grievance against the West, that was still alive and exploitable when that more peculiar to this earlier period, the claim for independence, could be said to have been almost settled. The totalitarian powers, whose anti-Semitism was, after all, the worst aggravation of the Jewish problem, nevertheless used every means to strengthen opposition to the democracies, and to stir up hatred and discord wherever possible. Events in Palestine intensified that mixed feeling of frustration and injustice that was the general outcome of the First World War. The Arabs became convinced that it was only possible to obtain justice by violence and they resorted to it, at first by insurrection and terrorism and later by organized warfare obstinately refusing that way of conciliation that Feisal and Weizmann had first tried to inaugurate in 1919.

These are the main lines of the history of the Arab revival during those twenty years: a revival that had lost it its high ideals, had impoverished the tone and scope of pan-Arab national aspirations, degrading them to particularist and regional ends, and had given a more and more harsh and niggardly character to a cause that, in its origin, aspired to such a noble breadth of vision.[1] The ideal of Arab unity was to be revived here and there; it reaffirmed itself more clearly and constructively after the Second World War, but by that time a political atmosphere had been created which drove the leaders irresistibly—though it was not openly admitted—towards personal power and dictatorship.

One must, however, beware of applying to this intermediate period, with its real gains for the Near East, judgement based on the more recent events. In order to retain perspective, we shall now pass in review the history of each of the Arab lands in the two troubled decades between the wars, and rather than give a detailed chronology of events, try to pick out the essential threads of their development.

Important changes took place during this period in the interior of the Arabian Peninsula which, according to King Husein's plan, should have been the core of a great united Arab state embracing all the ex-Ottoman provinces. The final Allied partition had not only put an end to this plan, but had left the King of the Hejaz entirely to his own resources just at the moment when a new enemy arose from within Arabia itself. This was the Wahabite Sultan of Nejd, Abdul Aziz ibn Saud, who during the previous twenty years had managed to reconstitute his ancestral power against rival emirs; with no pan-Arab ideas in his head, he had not moved a finger during the war to aid the Hashemite revolt, but had preferred to wait, and consolidate and extend his rule in the north and centre of Arabia as far as the confines of the Hejaz.

In 1924 King Husein, after having rejected a succession of proposed agreements with Britain that implied recognition of the new order in the Near East, made a new bid by proclaiming himself Caliph of all the Moslems, following the final abolition of the Turkish Caliphate. This was the signal for his ruin, since Ibn Saud at once started military action from the rival Wahabite State of Nejd against the Hejaz and in a few months

[1] See E. Rossi: *Documenti sull'origine e lo sviluppo della questione araba*, Rome 1944, p. xlvi.

destroyed the kingdom of the isolated Hashemite sovereign (1924–5). The champion of the Arab revolt, a victim partly of the disloyalty of others and partly of his own megalomania and rashness, spent the rest of his life bitterly and as an exile, first in Cyprus and later in Amman with his son Abdullah. While the fortunes of his family were budding anew outside Arabia, in Transjordan itself and in Iraq, the Saudi régime was firmly implanted in the Hejaz. It was to show itself the soundest and most dynamic power in the Peninsula, uniting two-thirds of it under the sceptre of Ibn Saud. Outside the 'Kingdom of Saudi Arabia' as the new state was named in 1932, there remained only the Yemen, ruled in medieval fashion by an 'Imam' of the Idrisite dynasty, and the various sultanates of South-eastern Arabia, all of them under British protection.

A little more than a century earlier the first expansion of the Wahabite puritans in Arabia had met with the disapproval and dismay of the orthodox Moslem world, which had seethed with indignation at seeing the Holy Places in the hands of these iconoclastic heretics (Mohammed Ali had then driven them out again in a bloodthirsty war, on the command of the Porte). But this time the prudence of Ibn Saud knew how to dispel such fears; he avoided a repetition of the former excesses in Mecca and Medina (the Wahabite doctrine does not admit the cult of saints or the construction of lavish memorials on their tombs) and he modified the full application of Nejdi austerity in the Hejaz.

The Arab state founded and firmly ruled by him for more than twenty years was in keeping both with the social conditions of the Peninsula and his own personal inclinations: a patriarchal Moslem state, combining absolute authority with the scrupulous observance of the tenets of Islamic public law as interpreted by Wahabite tradition. There was therefore nothing modern in this state, but rather reaction to the past; but to this archaic and primitive conception of the state, dedicated to a religious ideal and an internal despotism, Ibn Saud was able (and this was both his innovation and the reason for his success) to unite a gradual and deliberate acceptance of Western techniques and a cautious move towards social progress. This was explicit in the gradual reduction of nomadism, an attempt to tie the bedouin to the soil by the creation of agricultural colonies.

It later received an unexpected incentive through the discovery of oil in Arabia, which completely unsettled the old economic and social life of the Peninsula. The huge oilfields of Saudi Arabia began to be exploited from 1933 onwards by American capital (the Arabian-American Oil Company), with enormous consequences for at least that part of Arabia. Airlines, schools, hospitals, etc. came into existence by the consent, and at the same time under the watchful control, of the Saudi state. Western penetration was thus admitted within the strictly economic and technical field, but completely excluded in the political. The Saudi state, that is to say primarily the dynastic oligarchy in power, enriched itself without thereby losing effective control of the country.

This prudent policy, both conservative and progressive, traditional yet innovating, resulted in great prestige for the Saudi monarchy throughout the whole Arab, indeed all the Moslem, world. In those years when all the other Arab countries were fighting desperately to free themselves from Western tutelage, the jealously guarded independence of the desert Arab state shone like a symbol and an example, and led to a *rapprochement* between Saudi Arabia and those very states where the branches of the dispossessed Hashemite dynasty were reigning. Ibn Saud's expansion at the expense of other states was forgiven, and even in certain ways admired (as well as conquering the Hejaz, he had in 1934 fought a successful war against the Yemen for the possession of Asir), while his moderation and ordered firmness in the government of the Holy Places, and the organization of the Pilgrimage was approved. His rule was naturally based—and given the backward conditions of Arabia at the time it could not be otherwise —on the absolutism of the state. This became more evident after the death of its founder (1953), against whose heirs more open accusations of corrupt despotism have been made in recent years. But the moral capital accumulated by Ibn Saud (with perhaps some assistance from the material capital derived from oil royalties) has been great enough to uphold even a less enlightened administration.

The Hashemite dynasty, expelled from their fatherland the Hejaz, had been transplanted to the eastern arc of the Crescent, to the two states of Transjordan (renamed Jordan in 1948 after the Palestine war) and Iraq. The history of the former, at first an emirate and later (1946) a kingdom, ruled for the whole of this twenty-year period by the son of Husein, Abdullah, was, at least in those years, uneventful since its territory was mostly desert, with a mainly bedouin population and conditions of life not dissimilar to those of the Arabian Peninsula. Political life was restricted almost exclusively to the relations of the head of state and his circle with the mandatory power, of which King Abdullah was considered throughout all those twenty years as a faithful and well-subsidized dependent. This loyalty, even if it won him little love in fervid nationalist circles, none the less gave his state a period of tranquillity and security, maintained by the efficient Arab Legion, a military corps commanded by British officers, which showed itself the most reliable of all Arab units in the 1948 war. Transjordan gave Britain no headaches and was controlled as a means of land communication between the Mediterranean and the Persian Gulf.

Far more complex, eventful and at times dramatic was the history of near-by Iraq, where conditions were in some ways similar to those in Transjordan and Arabia, but whose development was complicated by the presence of large urban populations. Created as a separate state in 1921, its throne was given to Feisal, that son of Husein who had already been leader of the revolt in the desert and for a short time King of Syria before being expelled by the French. The friendship of Lawrence and Churchill and, as we have said, the qualms of conscience of the British for their conduct towards the Arabs, made this 'consolation' throne worth while, and he held it until his death (1933), showing great dignity, intelligence and active good will.

All sorts of serious problems weighed upon the new state, from the exact delimitation of its frontiers (the question of the territory of Mosul dragged on for many years; Turkey wanted it because of its oil, but in 1926 it was finally assigned to Iraq) to the treatment of its large and turbulent non-Arab minorities (Kurds and Assyro-Chaldeans). But the most important problem was always the relation with the mandatory power. The intrinsic ambiguity and precariousness of the mandate over states with a developed sense of nationality was felt by Britain herself, who tried to resolve it by substituting for it politico-military treaties that assured her a firm footing in the country while preserving at least a semblance of agreement. A whole series of such treaties was signed with Iraq (1922, 1926, 1927, 1930), the last of which transformed the mandate into a twenty-five year alliance that bound Iraq firmly to Great Britain in matters of foreign policy and the concession of military bases, but at the same time sanctioned the end of direct guardianship. In 1932, the mandate having officially ceased, Iraq was admitted into the League of Nations and began, though with these restrictions, her independent life but just at that time when his ability and balance were more than ever essential to the young Kingdom, Feisal, the ablest of the Hashemites, died.

Internal politics in Iraq, both before and after his death, were far from tranquil, being disturbed by clashes between various ethnic elements and religious creeds and the rivalries of different groups. Parliamentary life had indeed been introduced by the Organic Law of 1924 which had first given order to the country, but the lack of continued political education gave rise to frequent extra-parliamentary intrigues and coups. The military coups of 1936 and 1937 were particularly bloody, and in them various politicians lost their lives, including the Minister of War, Jafar al-Askari, who as an Ottoman officer had been one of the prime movers of the Arab revival and had later led the revolt alongside Feisal and Lawrence.

Great Britain, besides safeguarding her imperial line of communications, had been genuinely interested in the technical

91

progress of Iraq and in its civil and cultural evolution,[1] but despite it all, a fierce anti-British sentiment took root. A whole political faction arose in opposition to the pro-British party (one of whose leading apologists was Nuri al-Said, for many decades at the centre of Iraqi political life), giving rise to bigoted popular movements (in 1939, even the death of Ghazi, the son and successor of Feisal, in a motor-car accident, was attributed to the British) and culminating in the middle of the Second World War in the nationalist revolt of Rashid Ali al-Kailani.

But notwithstanding this instability, turbulence and sometimes even bloodshed, the twenty years between the wars were not without value for Iraq, since they procured for her, before all the rest of the former Ottoman provinces, three important advantages that served to offset internal disorders: the juridical position of a sovereign state, technical progress and dynastic continuity. The 'Arab Alliance Treaty' of 1936 with Saudi Arabia (the more significant because of the dispute between the ruling families of the two countries) at least marked a symbolic reminder of an homage to the pan-Arab ideals of the past and a faint presage for the future.

Like the British in Iraq, the French poured capital, administrative experience, cultural education and organization into the Lebanon and Syria, receiving for the most part only hatred and rebellion in return. The claim to rule poisoned all these benefits. Syria, already in the van of Arab nationalism, resented with especial bitterness the imperialist solution imposed by the victors, who had begun by dismembering her historic unity, by cutting off firstly Palestine and then the Lebanon (increased far beyond its mountainous core, to include all the Phoenician coastland and, in the interior, a large part of the former *vilayets* of Beirut and Damascus), and finally breaking up what remained into petty administrative units (Damascus, Aleppo, Jebel Druse, the Alaouite territory and the Sanjak of Alexandretta), all of which, with the exception of the last, were only merged into a single Syrian republic in 1936.

[1] Praiseworthy in the first years of the new state were the High Commissioner, Sir Percy Cox, and the archaeologist, Gertrude Bell.

The reason given for some of these subdivisions was the multiplicity of ethnic elements and above all of religious creeds, and the need for the protection of minorities—a classic excuse that has so often served as a pretext for the oppression of majorities. While Arab nationalism and irredentism was making every effort to break down the barriers between region and region in order to form a single and larger country, France was applying the contrary principle. General Gouraud, after expelling Feisal by force of arms, congratulated himself and the Syrians on having freed them from an attempt at Hejazi rule. Rebellion, which had long smouldered in Syria, exploded in the great Druse revolt of 1925, led by Sultan al-Atrash and supported by many groups from the cities.

French reaction, under General Sarrail, was particularly severe; Damascus was savagely bombarded, the Jebel Druse reconquered and the courts martial distributed sentences of death, imprisonment and exile. But the lesson served to teach the French the necessity of tempering force with persuasion; the military governors were replaced by civil commissioners and constitutional schemes were drawn up which, however, were all based on the mandate as an unchangeable premise. Only later, when she saw how much Britain had been able to do with Iraq, was there any thought of substituting for the mandate a politico-military Treaty of Alliance that would give at least formal satisfaction to Syrian nationalism while at the same time retaining for France substantial guarantees and privileges. But the Treaty to that effect which was drawn up in 1936 and approved by the Syrian Parliament was not approved by the French Assembly and remained inoperative up to the Second World War.

More peaceful, but still not without clashes, was the application of the mandate in the Lebanon, where the ties with France were older and stronger, since about half the population was Christian and very active missionary and educational work had been carried on there by Frenchmen. French had become almost a second national language in the Lebanon, and the Jesuit university of Beirut had for long been a living centre of

Western culture and science, alongside the American University. The French High Commissioner for the two countries lived in Beirut, and the Lebanese *élite* could be considered the most won over spiritually to the cause of permanent Franco-Levantine co-operation.

Despite all this, aspirations towards independence were becoming more and more evident in the Lebanon, though they were made as local as possible in order to preserve the balance of Christians and Moslems which would have been lost by a reabsorption of the Lebanon into Moslem Syria. The constitutions of 1926 and 1934 had granted the country democratic institutions, and the political struggle during those twenty years was tranquil and civilized by contrast with more recent events. Like Syria, Lebanon too had its own Treaty of Alliance in 1936, prelude to the end of the mandate, and again like Syria had to await another world cataclysm before the mandatory power could be forced really to relinquish its prey.

In the extreme north of Syria a special destiny was reserved for the territory of Alexandretta, illustriously Arab in tradition (it includes the shadow of what was once Antioch), but of mixed Arab-Turkish population. Since 1921 a Franco-Turkish agreement had assured to the Turkish minority the free use of their own language and the development of their own culture. Thenceforward Turkey staked a claim on the territory while the rights of Syria, that is of the Arabs, were entrusted to France, that mistress of 'divide and rule'. The separation of Alexandretta from the rest of Syria, with which it had historically always been united, was effected in 1939 by a proclamation of autonomy, the result of disputed elections, to which France finally agreed. The annexation by Turkey which followed in that same year was made under the threat of war in the summer of 1939 when France wanted to conciliate a possible ally by giving away with rather questionable right a part of the territory over which she had received a mandate. The cession of the zone of Alexandretta, renamed Hatay by the Turks, passed almost unnoticed in the turmoil of the world crisis but it has remained vivid in the memory and rancour of the Arabs and has appeared in recent times as a feature of their more ambitious nationalism.

The most discordant note in the history of the Near East between the two wars was sounded by Palestine. With its mixed (but, up to the end of the First World War, predominantly Arab-Moslem) population, its historical and religious traditions of importance to many faiths and many cultures, and its geographical position as a gateway to the Near and Middle East, this country seemed destined to be a bone of contention. During the First World War, the Husein-MacMahon correspondence (from which the British argued in vain that Palestine had been excluded) and the Balfour Declaration had created two contradictory premises, and their solution was thenceforward a matter of dispute between the mandatory power, the Arabs and the Jews. An impartial examination of the facts gives the impression that Britain was forced into this briar-patch more by thoughtlessness than by conscious perfidy, and then struggled desperately for nearly thirty years to get out of it again. It is true that Palestine was not mentioned in the British reservations about the projected Arab kingdom of Husein, but its omission at that time may simply have been due to forgetfulness.

A great deal more serious in its ambiguity was the positive proposal in the Balfour Declaration for a 'national home for the Jewish people' in Palestine; this formula did not necessarily mean a state (and there was no explicit mention of a state in the Feisal-Weizmann agreement), but the old Zionist ideals, revived by the increasingly tragic fate of Jewry in Europe, naturally tended to see it in this way and to define 'home' as a restored Hebrew state in Israel. In any case, Jewish immigration into Palestine began immediately after the war and rose dizzily in the second decade, with the advent of Nazism in Germany. In 1939 the Jews in Palestine already numbered half a million against a million Arabs, compared with the sixty thousand that they had been twenty years before!

Nor was this merely a question of a simple alteration of a numerical relation. In contrast to the Palestinian Arabs, still partly nomads, partly peasants and artisans, or indolent and backward landowners (the so-called *effendis*), the Jewish immigrants brought with them European technical skill in its most developed form, the capital and the will for profound agricultural and industrial changes, and an irresistible energy based, even more than on ancient patriotism, on the social and economic standards of contemporary Europe and America. The transfer of land from the Arabs to the Jews (organized in co-operatives and other collectives), was rapid and continuous and its consequences were quick to be felt in the primitive economy and new-born industry of Palestine. The local Arabs realized that without strenuous opposition the tide of Jewish immigration would rapidly submerge them; and they very soon began to protest, first by boycotts and by stirring up public opinion, and then by violence; while the Jews, strong in the Balfour Declaration and in the support of a great body of public opinion in the Anglo-Saxon countries, and later driven by the elemental need of escape from the inhuman persecutions in Central Europe, continued to stream into Palestine, felt by many of them to be the one sure haven.

The mandatory power, whose mandate was envied by no one, tried for the whole of these twenty years and even beyond to calm the emotions which it had so imprudently evoked. There were Arab risings in 1920, 1929, 1933, and most sanguinary of all, 1936–9. Britain had to reconcile the conflicting claims, on the one hand of the international Jewish Agency and the Palestine Vaad Leumi, and on the other of the Arab-Palestine Congress led by the Mufti of Jerusalem, Hajj Amin al-Huseini. Commission after commission of inquiry was sent to that tormented land, which (unique amongst all Arab regions of the Crescent) was deprived of any legal representative institutions, and governed *manu militari* until the end of the mandate.

The commission presided over by Lord Peel in 1937 was the first to put forward, amid the indignation of both sides, an open proposal for partition (with Jerusalem and some ports and air-bases reserved to England). This project was followed in 1938 by the London Round Table Conference between Jews and Arabs, which ended in failure because of the intransigence of both, and in 1939 by a fresh project, this time for an Arab-Jewish state with restrictions on immigration and further sales of land, a project substantially more favourable to the Arabs, but which they no less than the Jews were unwilling to accept. So the onset of the Second World War found the Holy Land of three religions (for Jerusalem is sacred also to the Arabs, because of the traditions and monuments that link it to the most venerated origins of Islam) harassed by civil war and repression and for the Arabs as a whole a living and painful symbol of what they considered flagrant European bad faith. In the words of Fouché: 'It was worse than a crime, it was a blunder', not to have foreseen from the first the reactions of a people accustomed for almost thirteen centuries to consider this land as their home, and now placed in contact with a people whose mentality, traditions and ways of life were alien to them, notwithstanding a basic ethnic-linguistic affinity between them and the undeniable claims of the Jews also to this historic land.

However, what in 1917 could and perhaps should have been avoided, had become an undeniable reality in 1939, made the more impossible to deny by the horrible excesses of racial intolerance and fanaticism that had in the meantime dishonoured Europe. No one could be in favour of refusing to a people persecuted and threatened with annihilation a refuge and the chance of a free and safe life in the land which had really once been theirs and whence their religious genius had shed an immortal light upon the world. This action, which had now become almost an international duty, still, however, involved an injustice towards a part of the Arab people, which in a climate of more goodwill and conciliation it might perhaps have been possible to mitigate by agreement. But neither the climate of 1939 nor that of the second post-war period were such as to permit the forces of goodwill and conciliation to succeed.

While in the Palestine problem the moral solidarity at least of the whole Arab world could be counted on, thanks mainly to the untiring efforts of the Mufti, elsewhere the struggle for independence stagnated and only Egypt was able, after a hard struggle of twenty years, to win liberty for herself. The declaration of independence of 1922 with its four reserved points, and the subsequent proclamation of the kingdom under Fuad, were only the first steps on a long road which it is worth considering more closely, because of the way in which the problems involved were interwoven, that is to say, *the* problem of foreign policy and those of internal policy. Egypt, at that time the only Arab country that had a political life of its own and an adequate development of parliamentary institutions, was involved in a three-cornered game, sometimes tense and dramatic, between the Crown, the political parties and the foreign power which paradoxically remained present in the country after having proclaimed its independence.

The leading figure in this game was King Fuad, who played a part which in many ways recalls that of Victor Emmanuel in the Italian *risorgimento*. He was just as desirous as any other Egyptian of attaining complete liberation from foreign influence but his own authority and prestige occupied his attention no less than the question of national independence. He did not hesitate to make use of extra-parliamentary intrigues and *coups de force*, for which his Piedmontese counterpart had not lacked the will, but merely the opportunity.

Confronting the Crown was an array of parties, some of them with little or no real following in the country. But at least one, the *Wafd*, had made itself initially very popular by its open defiance of Britain, and moreover had an exceptional leader in Zaghlul Pasha. The stature of this patriot exceeds by far that of his successors and imitators (compared to him, Nahas Pasha, for instance, was a merely consummate politician and demagogue), but his premature death left it uncertain how, after his first triumph, he would have conducted the rest of this difficult struggle. Egypt had other politicians of worth, however, even outside the *Wafd*, from which they had often withdrawn as a result of internal disputes or different political aims. Such were the severe and authoritarian, but honest, Mohammed Mahmud (chief of the Liberal Constitutionalists) or Ahmed Mahir (who in 1939 caused the secession of the 'Saadists' from the *Wafd*), or the energetic and able Ismail Sidky. It was a characteristic of Fascist propaganda in Italy before the war and is equally so of Nasser's dictatorship now, to depict the men and parties of those earlier decades as miserable, corrupt politicians, with paltry personal interests.

There may, in fact, be some truth in these accusations. But we must take into account the extremely difficult international situation, the constant pressure of the Crown and the British Residency, and the novelty for Egypt of a real parliamentary régime (the preceding assemblies had all been little more than consultative). Both parties and parliament knew how to react with dignity and success to the headstrong actions of the King, forcing him to retrace certain of his steps such as the abolition of the Constitution of 1923, which he replaced in 1930 by another and illiberal one, but which he was obliged to restore in 1935 under pressure from the *Wafd*.

Taken all in all, although the leaders of that party all seemed smaller men than its founder, and though as years went on it lost more and more of the initial popularity and prestige that he had won for it, it cannot be denied the merit of having carried on the struggle for independence with due respect for the wishes of the people and for parliamentary institutions (which could certainly not be said for the Crown and the puppet movements created by it, such as the court party of the 'Unionists') and of having by its energy, even if it was some-times demagogic, hastened the solution of the major national problem. Despite his lack of sympathy for constitutional government, Fuad worked assiduously and intelligently for the civil and cultural progress of the country, and pursued with a more balanced and modern spirit the tradition of his father, Ismail. That he should be condemned today by one who certainly could not give him lessons in democracy seems ironic.

The third party in all these contests was Britain, who after having had the country entirely in her hands, was naturally reluctant to loosen her grip; sometimes her excuses were in the name of civilization, but more often frankly in the name of her own imperial needs. None the less, *trahentibus fatis*, the grip was loosened and the prey finally abandoned.

Such was the background. The principal events were briefly as follows. The first elections of 1923 marked the triumph of the *Wafd* and the rise to power of Zaghlul Pasha, now returned from exile. But the work immediately begun by him in order to extend limitations of independence met with British resistance which, in the crisis of 1924 (assassination of the British Sirdar and consequent reprisals) stiffened into brute force. Zaghlul was forced to resign and died three years later without having returned to power, while a bitter duel was being fought between the temporizing Crown and the intransigent *Wafd*, now led by Nahas Pasha. Both he, when he was in power, and the leaders of the King's party (Mohammed Mahmud and later Sidky) who alternated with the *Wafd* in office, tried in vain to resolve the differences with Britain by negotiation. At the same time the King carried on his anti-democratic offensive with frequent dissolutions of the Chamber and the above-mentioned change of Constitution which did not, however, help to alleviate internal tension.

The struggle ended with the defeat of the Crown. In 1935 the Constitution of 1923 was re-established and the *Wafd* had another of its electoral victories in a plebiscite, which brought Nahas back to power. Shortly after, his determined adversary Fuad died, sincerely regretted by the Egyptian people who remembered his devotion to the moral and material welfare of the country rather than his political manœuvres. He was succeeded by his son, Farouk, whose fresh youth then attracted universal sympathy. Thus the *Wafd* supported by the greater part of public opinion, finally had a free hand to negotiate the Treaty of 1936 with Great Britain at a moment when the Ethiopian crisis had made her more conciliatory than usual. It was a decisive step by Egypt on the road to full independence.

By that treaty Britain at last consented to withdraw all her troops, concentrating them in limited numbers in the Canal Zone until Egypt should be in a position to take over her own defence. An effective Anglo-Egyptian Condominium over the Sudan (from which the Egyptian troops had been forced to retire in 1924) was again agreed to, and British support was promised for the abolition of Capitulations, which Egypt in fact obtained the following year by the Montreux Convention. On the other hand, it was linked with the usual twenty-year alliance, with an Egyptian obligation to place her bases and all her territory at the disposal of her ally in the event of a conflict. (In the Second World War this was given a burdensome interpretation.) But the essential was that three of the four 'reserved points' of 1922 were henceforth more or less eliminated, and that Egypt had come in sight of her legitimate ideal, to become mistress in her own house. Though critics of the Treaty were not lacking in Egypt itself, it was evident that national aspirations had taken a decisive step.

This was the culminating point of the *Wafd*. Under Nahas the party had almost brought to completion, despite very great difficulties, the work commenced by Zaghlul in 1919. But at the same time it marked the beginning of the descending curve of the party's fortunes, since it was now suffering the consequences of its own success. The new King showed as little sympathy towards the *Wafd* as his father had, and turned to the court favourite Mohammed Mahmud; but thenceforward the party no longer stood alone between the authoritarianism of the Crown and parliamentary democracy. Turbulent movements of Fascist type were already pullulating in Egypt and shirts of various colours began to appear in the market-places (the greens of 'Young Egypt' and the blues with which the *Wafd* tried to counter them). The government seemed to want to proceed energetically against them, but the totalitarian poison had long ago penetrated into the Nile Valley. The whole situation was 'frozen' during war conditions, but during the second post-war period, the poison was to become active again.

World War II and Fresh Groupings

World War II and Fresh Groupings

THE SECOND WORLD WAR surprised the Arabs more than half way between the complete servitude of the past and the complete liberty that still lay in the future. It found them embittered and disillusioned after this long struggle, prejudiced against the Allies and apt to look on the new conflict with a certain scepticism, since its ideological slogan, the struggle of liberty against tyranny, reminded them too much of the earlier one in which they had burned their fingers so badly. The cause of liberty seemed always to be personified in those Western democracies which had done so little to be worthy of it in the past twenty years and which were still encamped under arms on their soil. Of the enemies, Fascist Italy was certainly compromised by her imperialist policy in Libya and in Ethiopia but on the other hand vaunted a great understanding of the claims of the Arabs, the victims of 'Anglo-Jewish betrayal'. As for Germany, her alliance with the Ottoman oppressor was by now quite forgotten, and her immediate programme of making the former imperialists disgorge and of wiping out international Jewry (even though it might have the far from desired effect of making it flow even faster into Palestine) was not in itself distasteful to Arab nationalism.

Admittedly, the crimes of race-extermination and militarism of which the Nazis had been guilty even before the war should have alienated everybody who valued human dignity and decency in international affairs, even among the Arabs; but in the East also the process of disillusion that we have just described made the idea of totalitarianism less repugnant than it would have been a couple of generations before, and it even seemed to a few extreme nationalists that it was worth supporting the Axis cause if it meant hastening their own liberation.

On the other hand, the coming into force of the military treaties of alliance between Great Britain and certain Arab states like Iraq, Transjordan and Egypt, and the military occupation already existing in Palestine, and by the French in Syria, prevented the open adoption of a pro-Axis stand. All in all, the great majority of the Arabs remained passive spectators of the conflict, without enthusiasm or passion, emerging from that apathy only in sporadic attempts by impatient nationalists and, when the end could no longer be in doubt, in order to gain the maximum advantage for their cause.

Unlike the First World War, the Second brought few material struggles, privations and sorrows to the Arabs. Fighting again took place on Arab territory, but the central nucleus of the Arab world, Egypt and the Crescent, where the population was highest, was scarcely touched by the military operations and, finding itself this time entirely within the Allied sphere of action, did not know the shortages and the terrible famines that had raged there twenty-five years before.

At the beginning of the war the *Armée d'Orient* of General Weygand was concentrated in Syria and the neighbouring countries. This force was supposed to cover the Levant from German attacks, but after the French collapse and the armistice with Germany it was dissolved without firing a shot. In the following year (spring of 1941) a timely Anglo-Gaullist action freed Syria and the Lebanon from dependence on Vichy and restored them to the Allies. It was then that General Catroux, in the name of Free France, made both these countries a solemn declaration of independence (which the unratified treaties of 1936 should have granted), though it was to be provisionally limited by the necessities of war. But when these two peoples showed that they intended to take these declarations literally and that no reference to, or recognition of, the mandate was to be included in the new constitutions, the France of de Gaulle did not show itself any more liberal than that of Sarrail. In November 1943 the Commissioner, Helleu, intervened forcibly in the Lebanon, arrested the President and his ministers, suspended the constitution and took other drastic measures. The crisis was resolved by British intervention, but it certainly did not serve to make the peoples of Syria and the Lebanon any more attached to France.

Meanwhile in Iraq, Britain too had to repress an outbreak of Arab nationalism; in the spring of 1941 an ex-Prime Minister Rashid Ali al-Kailani, recovered power by a *coup* and forced the Regent, Abdul Illah, with the boy-king Feisal II, and other pro-English political leaders, to fly the country. This was the boldest step attempted in Arab territory in favour of the Axis; Axis aid was invoked and openly accepted. A chorus of hosannas to Arab liberty resounded from the microphones of Axis propaganda, and the figures of al-Kailani and the Mufti, Amin el-Husseini, who supported him with his usual rabid anti-English hatred, became celebrated among the 'liberators of the peoples' in Rome and Berlin. But the material aid which the Axis could give was limited to a few occasional aeroplanes, whereas a prompt convergence on Iraq of British-led troops soon ended the rebellion after a few weeks of unequal struggle. The Regent, with the King and the other exiles, returned (while Rashid Ali and the Mufti in their turn sought refuge in Italy) and Iraq aligned itself docilely alongside Great Britain, declared war on the Tripartite Powers in 1943 and awaited a more suitable moment to press its claims.

Egypt was to know a real war of manœuvre between the Commonwealth and the Axis forces on her western frontier, a war that at one time threatened to overwhelm her. The fluctuations of the North African campaign are well known, beginning with the Italian advance to Sidi Barrani (summer 1940), the Wavell offensive (December 1940), which took the British as far as the Gulf of Syrte, and Rommel's first counter-offensive which drove them back to the Egyptian frontier; then the fresh offensive of Auchinleck (January 1942) which took the British forces painfully up to Benghazi and the overwhelming Italo-German action of the following spring which penetrated deeply into Egyptian territory only to be brought to a halt at al-Alamein, ninety-four miles from Alexandria. And finally the decisive battle in October of that year (1942) that took its name from al-Alamein, in which Montgomery finally eliminated the Axis peril to Egypt and began the victorious British advance along the African coast, which ended the following spring when the British forces joined up with the Americans in Tunisia.

All that need be mentioned here are the effects and counter-effects of the war on Egypt, the political attitude of that country and its relations with England during these years. Egypt had scarcely garnered the first fruits of the Treaty of 1936, with the commencement of the military evacuation towards the Canal and the abolition of the Capitulations, when the new conflict once again placed her in the hands of Great Britain and exposed her to all the risks, injuries and dangers of war. The military clauses of the Treaty were loyally observed (it would have been difficult to do anything else) but were accompanied by resistance to a complete political identification with the cause of the Allies.

The cabinet presided over by Ali Mahir at first refused to declare war on Italy and insisted on a policy of neutrality. There was for some time the paradox of an 'independent' and neutral country on whose territory war was being waged between one of its allies and that ally's enemy and receiving from the skies bombs intended for the ally. The neutralism of Ali Mahir, which was inspired not so much by any positive sympathy for the Axis as by uncertainty as to what turn events were likely to take, was forced to give way before British pressure. He was dismissed and kept under house-arrest. But until the autumn of 1942 there was certainly more than one person in Egypt, held back by the occupation forces, the police and the censorship, who in his innermost heart was willing to throw in his lot with the Germans. We do not know the private thoughts of King Farouk; but in February 1942, under the threat of British tanks, he had to agree to recall Nahas and the *Wafd* once more to office. They, by a new paradox, were to give full support to the British in a policy of conciliation.

It would be curious to know what parts all these actors in the drama might have played, Axis liberators and liberated Egyptians alike, if Rommel's thrust in the spring of 1942 had been successful and if Egypt, which had already been guaranteed integrity and independence from the Italo-German side at the same time as a régime of military occupation was being prepared, had been able to sample a change of masters. But this interesting experiment was not to take place, and a few months after al-Alamein the imperial dreams of the 'have-nots' collapsed for ever, while even for the 'haves' it was now too late to turn back the years and the fates.

The battle in the desert in that decisive autumn of 1942 really marked the turning of the tide for the free world, quite beyond the problems and aspirations of the Arabs; but for them also, this time, it was not a disappointment. As well as saving Egypt from the covetousness of the Axis, it created the conditions for the keeping of another promise, the one promise made in this war by Britain to the Arabs—a promise, incidentally, at some-one else's expense. In January 1942, Eden had paid homage to the military aid furnished to the Allied cause by the Senussi leader Mohammed Idris, an exile from Cyrenaica then in Egypt, and his Arab-Libyan forces, and had given a pledge not to permit the return of Italy to Cyrenaica; a pledge that was kept in full. Meanwhile, as far as Egypt was concerned, no reasonable politican any longer dreamt of backing a loser and the assassination in February 1945 of the Prime Minister, Ahmed Mahir (brother of Ali), after he had at last made Egypt declare war on Germany, appears not so much an extreme-right-wing protest as an act of lunacy.

As the war rolled to an end grinding down Nazi-Fascist imperialism, and the people began to dare to hope for the triumph of the ideals of liberty and justice, the first Arab dream of unity that had been stifled by the more urgent task of liberation, began once more to appear. Having broken the Ottoman Empire into various regional states, the victors of the First World War hoped to obtain a more docile administration, and to take advantage of the geographical and historical characteristics of individual regions; they had preferred to accentuate what divided them rather than what united them. This had indeed deepened the regional differences in the intervening twenty years but could not prevent the development of other plans to overcome these divisions. Such plans were primarily fostered to serve dynastic ambitions, and it is significant that they first found expression in the lands ruled by two branches of the Hashemite dynasty.

In 1941, the Emir, as he was then, of Transjordan, Abdullah, favoured the idea of a 'Greater Syria' which should unite (naturally under his sceptre) Syria, the Lebanon, Palestine and Transjordan as in the great days of the Caliphate. In the following year the Iraqi statesman Nuri al-Said took up and extended this project,[1] even looking forward to the time when this same 'Greater Syria' would be finally integrated into an 'Arab Union' with Iraq. But distrust and resistance at once appeared; from Syria itself and from the Lebanon, both of which feared to lose their national individuality within a larger unit (in the Lebanon with understandable anxiety for the balance of the two religions, which had always been scrupulously maintained), from Saudi Arabia, because of the flaming up once more of the old rivalry with the Hashemites, and from Egypt, still closed within her narrow regionalism and caring nothing for larger Arab unities beyond her own frontiers.

The times were not yet ripe for true political 'unions'. But the advantages of co-ordination among the various Arab states appeared so evident in view of the overlapping problems of the war that was drawing near its close, that they induced even Egypt to sponsor an inter-state organization that would safeguard national sovereignties and at the same time unite them for the common interest (on the lines of a *Staatenbund* rather than a *Bundesstaat*). Such was the origin of the 'Arab League', created with the support of Britain in the euphoria of the imminent Allied victory, while the Arab states of the East, by a chain declaration of war on Germany, assured themselves places in the General Assembly of the United Nations.

The initiative for the formation of the League was thus taken by the country which had until then remained cold and hostile to plans for the fusion of the Fertile Crescent. After a

[1] Nuri al-Said had put forward this plan as early as 1931, so that he might well be called its author. It was then taken up anew and fostered by the Emir Abdullah until his death.

preparatory conference in Alexandria in the autumn of 1944, the formal inauguration of the League, the 'Society of Arab States' (*Jamiat al-Duwal al-'Arabiyya*) took place in Cairo on 22nd March, 1945. It included Egypt, Saudi Arabia, Iraq, Syria, Lebanon, Transjordan and, a little later on, the Yemen. The League was declared an association of independent and sovereign Arab states formed in order 'to strengthen relations between members, to organize political plans aimed at collaboration among them, to protect their independence and integrity and generally to discuss the affairs and interests of the Arab world'.

Because of these stipulations of independence and sovereignty, to all intents and purposes achieved, though legally still pending for certain members like Syria and the Lebanon, it could not immediately invite the votes of Tunisia, Libya and Morocco, but all of these entered one by one as they attained independence. But Palestine was still lacking for the whole Arab group of the East to be complete, and since the burning problem of Palestine was the most pressing for a pan-Arab understanding, a special clause was added to the Pact whereby Palestine, in expectation of its long-desired independence, had the right to a delegate in the Council of the League. The League's administrative organs were the Council of Representatives of the individual associated states, Commissions of Study, and the Permanent Secretariat in Cairo.

The formation of this first associated pan-Arab organization excited great enthusiasm and high hopes in those who saw in it a move towards the union of the various dispersed members of the Arab world. In reality its capacity for action turned out to be considerably more limited than had been hoped. It was of real value where the common interest of all its members was concerned (though even here, as events with regard to Israel showed, more in the field of diplomacy than of arms), but when the interests of individual states diverged, it showed itself unable to reconcile them. None, in fact, was genuinely disposed to sacrifice its own sovereignty (new for many of them), its own sentiments and resentments and particularist plans to a federal ideal.

The Arab Revival

In its first years, the League experienced a bitter checkmate and a progressive weakening. The checkmate was in Palestine where the whole Arab world had decided to engage itself to the utmost; the weakening is shown by the whole later history of the Eastern Arab states in the post-war period, which, as we shall see, did not develop along the lines laid down by the League, but often directly contrary to them. On the other hand, early political successes were not lacking, mainly in the aid given to individual Arab countries in the post-war period to obtain their full independence. Thus it effectively supported the requests of Syria and the Lebanon in the United Nations for the final withdrawal of French troops; it fought tenaciously and succeeded in preventing any return of Italy to Libya, over and above the British pledge which only concerned Cyrenaica; it supported the liberation of Tunisia and Morocco from French tutelage and it worked for the cessation of British rule in the Sudan and the reunion of that country with Egypt (this last only partially achieved).

But the activities of the Arab League were from the start not intended to be limited to the purely political field, but to cover economic, cultural and social questions also; and here its balance-sheet shows considerably greater credits. In its two annual sessions, in certain extraordinary sessions and in the pan-Arab meetings and congresses organized by it, it passed a whole series of important measures, unifying and simplifying procedures affecting its various members; questions of commercial exchanges, customs dues and currencies, communications and passports, extradition, hygienic and quarantine agreements were debated and thrashed out between individual Arab states under the aegis of the League, as they certainly could not have been in separate negotiations, and contributed appreciably to the civil and social progress of the Arab countries.

In addition, really praiseworthy work was carried out by a Committee of the League in co-ordinating the cultural energies and ideas of individual states, by debating problems of common interest (first and foremost that of the language) and creating a magnificent study-centre in the Institute of Manuscripts, which is now recording on microfilm the treasures of medieval Arab literature from all the Near and Middle East, and also from Europe. In this field pan-Arab solidarity has been able to express itself to the full in the study and appreciation of the heritage of its ancestors, which the Arabs have learnt from Europe how to study scientifically. Arab universities have been founded on the European model at Baghdad, Damascus, Beirut; no less than four in Egypt, two in Cairo, one in Alexandria, one in Assyut and one at Rabat in Morocco, besides Arab language academies in Cairo and Damascus. Those who recall the cultural and scientific backwardness of the Arab world only a few decades before (notwithstanding the efforts of the pioneers of the nineteenth and early twentieth centuries), will recognize the immense distance travelled in more recent years, *viribus unitis*, under the impulse and on the example of Europe.

A great share of the merit for this progress must go to the League and to the new consciousness of unity which it expressed, though in a hesitant and faltering way. But on the other hand, after more than twenty years of regional loyalties, none of the members of the League had the will and the courage to break with every form of particularism in the political field and return to the ardour of the ideas of unity that had originally inspired the revival. Perhaps it was too much to expect the generosity and boldness that would have been needed to overcome these difficulties. (for example the great disparities of economic and social conditions between the Arabian Peninsula and the more advanced countries of the Crescent, to say nothing of Egypt), but the lack of them prevented the achievement of larger groupings and fusions by free agreement. These were achieved later, but by quite different means, under the dynamic force of totalitarianism and the reaction to it.

Even if with the passing of time the League showed itself to be a less solid and efficient creation than it had at first appeared, the Arab world none the less emerged from the Second World War, in which it had struggled and suffered so much less, incomparably better off than from the First. It emerged from it above all freed from that complex of inferiority towards Europe, whose primacy was more and more shattered by recent events; the real victors of the new conflict, already confronting one another as rivals, were in fact two powers geographically and spiritually outside Europe. The feared and hated Britain, though she too was formally a victor, was already in the second rank when compared with these two, while her empire was either disintegrating or reforming itself into fresh relationships of states and peoples; as to France, her status as a victor in name only was evident to every unprejudiced observer.

Instead of being merely the object of negotiations and seeing their representatives lobbying and being rebuffed by the arbiters of peace, the Arab peoples now saw the Great Powers full of smiles and benign promises, negotiating with their heads of state as equals, saw their new groupings greeted with sympathy and their representatives sitting alongside the Europeans in the new assembly of the United Nations. All this signified, or ought to have signified, that the times of colonialism, the 'white man's burden', were for ever over, and that the West had at least resigned itself to negotiate with the Eastern peoples on a basis of parity.

This naturally was a continuous process, which is still going on. There was still some resistance to be overcome, some trouble-spots to be pacified, before the success could finally be claimed. Whereas Great Britain showed, generally speaking, a more immediate goodwill and good faith in demobilizing the trappings of war in Egypt and in Iraq (we shall speak of Palestine a little later on), France was rather more reluctant to do the same in the Lebanon and Syria, even though the full independence of these countries had several times been proclaimed and guaranteed. It had to come to violent bazaar riots in Beirut and Damascus in May 1945 before the French government, under energetic British pressure, resigned itself to total military withdrawal. This was completed by the end of 1946, and from that date the two states of the Levant definitely emerged from French tutelage. France had given them moral and material benefits, first among them the light of modern education and the thirst for liberty; but as these benefits had come to them mingled with ills, almost inextricably combined, so remembrance and gratitude, if indeed they existed, were quickly swamped by waves of fresh passions.

While Egypt went back to the situation of 1936 and initiated the final phase of her liberation, a new Arab state was born on her western frontiers. 'Sated' Italy, having rashly allied herself with 'hungry' Germany to fight and lose a ruinous war, handed back both old and new acquisitions, some being lands in which she had only carried out the work of civilization and others in which her only interest had been prestige and exploitation. We have already noted that England had given a pledge to the Senussi not to permit Italy to return to Cyrenaica, where the reconquest in the Fascist style of 1930 had left bitter memories. But for Tripolitania, where this pledge did not hold, a long diplomatic skirmishing took place in which it seemed for a moment (Bevin-Sforza agreement of 1948) that Italy might be able to return with a mandate to prepare the country for independence; but the active propaganda of the Arab League and the little sympathy upon which Italy could count in the first post-war years, frustrated this plan. In 1950 the United Nations sanctioned the creation of a united Libyan state in federal form (Tripolitania, Cyrenaica and Fezzan) and this was inaugurated under the rule of the Senussi Mohammed Idris at the end of 1951. If we have here anticipated the formation of the kingdom of Libya, it is because this may be considered one of the direct consequences (even if some years delayed) of the Second World War, whereas the rebellion of all remaining French North Africa is a more indirect and distant consequence of it. In the immediate post-war period, the question of North African independence still seemed the concern of the restless few and might well have been thought much farther away from maturity than was actually the case.

But always unsolved, burning and urgent for all the Arab world, at the end as at the beginning of the war, was the

Palestine problem. The first years of the war had seen a sort of truce imposed on Arabs and Jews by the arts and arms of England. But when the Jewish demands for a real and effective state of Israel took shape, affairs took a turn for the worse.

From 1943 onwards, up to the effective partition of 1948, British policy, which had always been accused by the Arabs of favouring the Jews, seemed to make an about-turn; it was rather America who supported the Zionist demands more and more openly, while the mandatory power tried to modify them by placing obstacles in the way of the incessant flow of immigrants, even by drastic methods, and thus drawing down upon it the anger of the Jewish extremists.

These showed themselves just as capable as the Arabs of violence and terrorism, as was proved by the notorious Stern Gang (an offshoot of Irgun Zvai Leumi, a Jewish military organization in the service of Zionist ideals); between 1944 and and 1946 this gang committed a chain of murders and acts of terrorism, both in Palestine and outside. One of the victims was the British Minister of State for the Near East, Lord Moyne. On another occasion the British Headquarters in Jerusalem, the King David Hotel, was destroyed by a Stern Gang bomb, causing many deaths. But the most illustrious victim of Jewish terrorism after the creation of the State of Israel was Count Bernadotte, the envoy of the United Nations who lost his life in the noble attempt to conciliate the two parties in this conflict. The Arabs, needless to say, did not in the meantime lag behind, either in or outside Palestine; and 1945 saw many Arab countries, above all Libya, immersed in internal conflict and bloodshed.

The Arabs, who had gained much from the Second World War as a tardy recompense for the disappointments of the First, not only obtained the recognition of some basic rights, but were spurred on to the intolerant and often violent pursuit of other rights to which they considered themselves entitled, and which still seemed to them to be delayed. The callousness and pitiless brutality which every war brings in its train, but in which the last war certainly excelled over all the others, seemed to lead to a brutalization of the methods adopted by governments towards their subjects and towards each other, in spite of the brave ideals of inter-racial tolerance that were being encouraged by the new world-assemblies. The later histories of the Arab peoples and states shows how they, until yesterday the victims of the violence of others, did not hesitate in their turn to imitate their oppressors.

Problems of the Post-War Period

Problems of the Post-War Period

THE LATEST PHASE OF THE HISTORY of the Arab peoples, which began after the end of the Second World War and is still going on, reflects the confusion caused by the new power-groupings in the world. The immense progress made by the Arabs in national status compared with their pre-war situation has given them an arrogant and perhaps exaggerated idea of their own power and a restless drive to prove it in the realization of further aims. At the present these are: (1) a radical solution to the problem of Israel (which in reality appears somewhat remote), (2) the liquidation of the last vestiges of the colonial system (Algeria), (3) the maintaining of a position of vantage, one might almost say of fence-sitting, between America and Russia, and, finally, (4) Arab unity, which depends on the solution of all the preceding problems.

Such are the major objectives of foreign policy, but alongside them are other urgent and equally grave problems of internal policy which cut across them: economic stability, social disputes, the choice of authoritarian methods or civil liberties. Postponing until the last chapter the problem of Arab unity, in which there have recently been striking developments, we will now review the other problems in a brief account of the last thirteen years.

The dominant trend of this period has been nationalism of the most rigid and insular kind. The nineteenth century conception of nationality as part of a common brotherly progress has been lost in contemporary Arab propaganda and its place taken by a completely unbalanced idea of nationalism. To the old resentments against colonial exploitation are now added resentments which picture the Arabs as still continuously besieged by Western imperialism. Here too the same complicated process has been repeated in the East that the West had known after national union had been achieved—the degeneration of patriotism into nationalism, of the thirst for liberty and independence into that for expansion and domination.

But what distinguishes the Arab and non-Arab East from the West in this process, and this is not to the advantage of the Arabs, is that while in the West, since the end of the nineteenth century, the restraints of liberal-democracy and socialism have balanced the nationalist impulse, there are no such restraints in the contemporary Middle East. Everywhere democracy is a thin façade (where it has not already collapsed) covering more or less self-confessed authoritarian régimes, ruling by naked force. Liberty remains a popular watchword, but it means only one thing: liberty from the foreigner, which is rightly or wrongly always stated to be in danger. Internal liberty is stifled; every dissident voice silenced. Even dissidence itself (as the most recent case of the Lebanon appears to prove) is based more on personal rivalries and internal squabbles than on ideals. Social-ism, on the other hand, the great voice of justice and humanity raised throughout the West against the follies of nationalism, was for long not a moving force in the history of the Near East. Nationalism has smothered it, sometimes persecuting it by police methods, but more often trying to conciliate it and draw it on to the same side in the fight against Western intervention.

In this it has been aided by the recent trends in Soviet policy. The Soviet Union, after a policy of clandestine provocation and sabotage against the *bourgeois* classes and parties in the East, has in the second post-war period accepted Arab nationalism as a weapon against the West, backing its claims to the full and apparently ignoring the question of the class struggle. The paradoxical position has thus arisen of a Communist state whose creed is material progress supporting socially backward, or capitalist tyrannies. Not for the first time in history, political expediency has overridden social conviction and religious faith. These same champions of the liberty of the peoples, who have extinguished the state and perhaps the actual inhabitants of the Moslem Tatars in the Crimea, have not stinted their support for other Moslem peoples when they happened to be useful to them in the 'cold war' against the West.

Post-war Arab nationalism has thus been able to play a profitable double game, asking and accepting economic and political aid from both sides, and flirting ever more openly with the Communist bloc without making any corresponding reform of their society. These economic and social problems of the contemporary Arab states are in fact unsolved and have been neglected in favour of the demands of foreign policy; and if profound social reforms have not up to the present been carried out in the states openly aligned with the Communist bloc, how much less can they be expected from those that are philo-capitalist, like the Lebanon or Jordan, or from that still 'feudal' Saudi Arabia? The history of socialism in the Near East is not only still to be written, it is indeed yet to be made, however enthusiastically the oligarchies in power may profess admiration for its ideas.

The first great problem of the post-war period for the Arab League was the Palestine imbroglio, the main outlines and earlier stages of which have already been described. The League itself was created with a solemn obligation to solve this problem in the way desired by the Arabs, that is by the ending of Jewish immigration, the withdrawal of the British and the recognition of the Arab character of Palestine. But in the years immediately following, events developed in a manner contrary to Arab hopes, although Great Britain, under whose aegis Israel had been born, was evidently lessening her support for Zionism. The Jews had long won a firm foothold in the country by both legal and illegal immigration. They had military organization, and they were preparing for the final consolidation as soon as the British occupation ended.

Great Britain, sick of war, submitted the solution of the Palestine problem to the United Nations in 1947. This took the form of partition into two states, Arab and Jewish, politically distinct but economically associated. This last point should have been mutually beneficial but it needed the goodwill and co-operation of two implacable enemies. Partition was sanctioned by the General Assembly of the United Nations of 27th November, 1947, and the end of the mandate, fixed for

1st August, 1948, was anticipated by Great Britain on 15th May.

On that date the Arabs and the Jews ought to have carried out the partition which assigned to the Arabs Central and Eastern Palestine (Samaria and Judaea, except Jerusalem, which was to be demilitarized and internationalized), Western Galilee and a strip of the southern coastline with its centre at Gaza; and to the Jews Eastern Galilee, the coastal plain with the ports, and the Negev. But these boundaries remained theoretical; to make them a fact required force. While on 14th May the Jewish National Council (Vaad Leumi) proclaimed the state of Israel at Tel-Aviv, the Arab states of the League (Syria, the Lebanon, Transjordan, Iraq and Egypt) invaded the territory of Palestine in accordance with the threats that they had made and the pledge that they had taken.

The war in the field was short and at once revealed the military inadequacy of the Arabs, whose only efficient force was the Jordan 'Arab Legion' commanded by Glubb Pasha and other British officers. It thrust beyond the Jordan into Samaria and Judaea, and was able to hold the city of Jerusalem, preventing the Jews from penetrating eastward. But everywhere else the Arab forces were driven back by the energetic Jewish counter-offensive, which over-ran Galilee, Southern Judaea with Beersheba, and the Negev. The United Nations immediately dispatched the Bernadotte mission, which after some weeks succeeded in obtaining a cease-fire, and in the first half of 1949 (after Bernadotte himself had been murdered) a series of armistices was concluded between Israel and the individual Arab states that still determine the precarious frontiers and even more precarious relations between the contestants.

The frontiers remained those, broadly speaking, of the projected partition, improved to Israel's advantage by the total acquisition of Galilee (almost the whole of the Lake of Tiberias is now in Israeli territory, but bristling with military equipment and posts and menaced on the east by the proximity of the Syrian frontier) and of the southern zones which were in Israeli

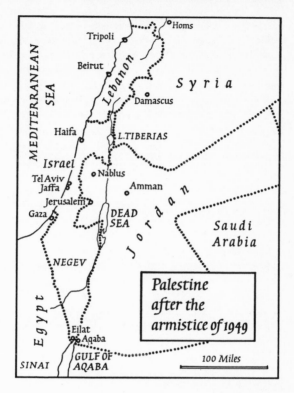

Palestine
after the
armistice of 1949

100 Miles

hands at the time of the armistice. The city of Jerusalem has remained cut in two, and barbed wire and machine-guns dominate the Holy Places of the three religions. In keeping with the spirit of this strange age of undeclared wars and armistices of indefinite duration which take the place of peace, men under arms face one another in enmity across the dismembered land of Jesus Christ.

The military and political failures of the Palestine action had profound repercussions in all the Arab lands, revealing technical and political imperfections, for which as usual scapegoats were sought. The commissariat was corrupt; the organization of military supplies in disorder; political co-ordination insufficient; and the armies badly trained and lacking in fighting spirit. The Jews, on the other hand, were efficient, strong in European technical knowledge and animated by a higher spirit of idealism and sacrifice. A tide of bitterness and frustration over-flowed from the inglorious Palestine campaign, dimming the joy of recently acquired liberties. The unity of the League was put to a severe test, most of its members remaining rigidly intransigent towards Israel, while the one Arab state which had gained some profit from the war, Transjordan, was more inclined to negotiation. Its most serious social effect had been the creation of a mass of Arab refugees (almost a million) who had fled from Palestine and sought refuge in the neighbouring lands. Before agreeing to a partial return to their native places or to any other plan for settling them the Israelis have always insisted on the conclusion of a peace treaty, and to this the Arabs have not yet been able to resign themselves. Transjordan then proceeded, unilaterally and against the wishes of the other members of the League, to annex the territories occupied by her on the other side of the Jordan (1st December, 1948) and a few months later (26th April, 1949) proclaimed the Hashemite kingdom of Jordan. The Arabs have been reduced to a policy of ineffectual siege and petty economic boycott against Israel, thus perpetuating a zone of international friction that may at any time flare up into open conflict, with unforeseeable results.

In the autumn of 1956, at the same time as the Suez crisis and more or less fortuitously coupled with it, there was an Israeli military sortie southwards, which both confirmed the impression of evident Israeli military superiority and at the same time the extreme delicacy of balance in the region. The sortie led to the Israeli occupation of Gaza which had been in Egyptian hands since 1948, and to an easy military promenade into Sinai, which the Israelis evacuated only after the intervention of the United Nations and the threats of the Soviet Union. The Palestine problem seems destined to be one that our generation will never see solved.

The young Jewish state, which celebrated its tenth anniversary in an atmosphere of faith and hard-working enthusiasm, is thus a perpetual source of irritation to the Arab world, which, however, seems determined against a compromise solution. At the base of this attitude is a feeling of bitterness for an injury suffered, and there are valid historical and social reasons to justify it. But today, since it is obvious that Israel can neither be ignored nor annihilated, except by some apocalyptic world convulsion, wisdom and common sense should counsel the Arabs to accept the *fait accompli* and obtain from a policy of co-operation and good neighbourliness what hatred has been powerless to obtain. This truth is very probably privately realized by more than one Arab, but no Arab politician has had the courage to defy unpopularity and expose himself to the reprisals of terrorism by pronouncing it. An agreement with Israel could be the surest indication of the ascendancy of new forces of good sense and goodwill in the Arab world which seems today to be entirely in the grip of irrationality and passion.

The unfortunate contest with Israel and its political and social consequences has been only one of the reasons for the chronic restlessness of the more recent history of the Near East. Another permanent reason is the preoccupation, one might almost say the national obsession, with the eradication of every trace of colonialism. Colonialist intentions and intrigues are suspected in every agreement and co-operation with the West. Let us not deny that in both the ex-colonial Western powers colonialism has been, and still is, hard to kill (we shall see this in the Maghreb question), but it is certain that the mistrust shown by large sections of Arab public opinion has sometimes taken on almost pathological forms. It can be explained only by a complex of resentments over the past that recent events have unhappily served to revive.

Iraq offers a striking example of this exasperated sensitiveness. When in 1948 the Foreign Minister, Salih Jabr, negotiated a renewal of the 1930 Treaty of Alliance with Great Britain, on a basis indubitably more favourable to Iraq, the remaining military concessions still granted to the British excited public opinion to such an extent that the new Treaty was not only not ratified but its negotiator was forced to flee abroad in peril of his life.

More recently Anglo-Iraqi relations took on a new form in the much-discussed 'Baghdad Pact', which pan-Arab nationalism regarded as a return of British imperialism to the Near and Middle East, but which to a more impartial observer is what it appears to be, an essentially defensive arrangement. Its nucleus was the direct agreement between Iraq and Turkey (drawn up at Baghdad in February 1955), with which Iran and Pakistan associated themselves. In April, Great Britain also signed a specific agreement with Iraq within the ambit of the Pact. It formed a defensive zone in the Near and Middle East as an anti-Soviet precaution, to check any threat from the North. Great Britain organized it, no longer to defend an India already lost, but to preserve a balance in the Near East and above all to maintain free access to the precious oilfields. The adhesion of Iraq to a British-sponsored Pact was felt by the rest of the Arab world as a defection and as a serious crack in the Arab unity of action foreshadowed in the League. But it is sufficient to note that countries as jealous of their independence and national sovereignty as Turkey and Pakistan were involved in the Baghdad Pact, in order to refute the 'colonialist' interpretation.

The man who had led Iraq to such agreements with Great Britain and who had always followed a pro-British policy was the old leader, Nuri al-Said, who had dominated the Iraqi political scene from the distant beginnings of the Arab revolt against the Turks down to our own days. Repeatedly accused of despotism and corruption and in fact far from exemplary in his methods of internal policy, wherein he exercised a disguised dictatorship, this clever politician had ended by becoming the *bête noire* of pan-Arab extremism, though in the past many of the schemes for uniting the Fertile Crescent under Hashemite hegemony had been originated by him. A real step in that direction had just been taken by the Iraqi-Jordan federation of February 1958 when the bloody *coup d'état* of July brought down the monarchy in Iraq and overthrew the old statesman (see page 164). His crime was his co-operation with the West, and having remained only half-way along the road to dictatorship. The drama of Baghdad showed the world both the present level of Iraqi civilization and also the extreme fragility and unpreparedness of a parliamentary dictatorship of the old style when faced with the methods of modern totalitarianism. Not one of the dictators whom humanity had suffered and still suffers, ever let himself be taken by surprise with the ease of that 'dog of the imperialists', Nuri al-Said.

The policy of the other Hashemite state, Transjordan, was dominated up to his tragic death, by the personality of King Abdullah, the last to remain on the scene from the times of the Arab Revolt of Husein and Lawrence. For three decades this sovereign, guided by a persistent expansionist ambition, advanced from a petty Emir to be a King and from supervising a desert to ruling a large and fertile state on both banks of the Jordan. We have already seen how he was the only one of the Arabs to gain anything from the war with new-born Israel and how he unscrupulously incorporated his territorial gains even at the risk of a rupture with the other Arab states. It is not too much to suppose that if the Arab-Israel dispute could have been limited to Jordan, he would in time have found some compromise, notwithstanding or perhaps because of the fact that Jordan was weighed down by the greatest number of the Palestine refugees (about half a million), to whom she alone has extended the rights of citizenship.

In his enlarged kingdom of Jordan, Abdullah continued to foster the dream of the union of the Fertile Crescent for which his father had come out of his desert homeland. He thus threatened Syrian and Lebanese regionalism and exasperated the anti-Jewish extremists by the possibility of his coming to an agreement with Israel. The end came with his assassination in Jerusalem (20th June, 1951) carried out, it seems, by an emissary of the Mufti of Jerusalem, Amin al-Huseini. After the brief reign of his son the Anglophobe and unbalanced Talal, the latter was succeeded on the throne of Jordan by his son Husein, who has not hesitated on the one hand to satisfy nationalism at home by dismissing Glubb Pasha and the other British officers, and on the other to consolidate relations with Iraq, until July 1958 deviationist and pro-Western, surmounting repeated international crises and thus coming even more into conflict with Syria and Egypt.

The post-war history of Syria has been the most stormy and unfortunate in the whole Fertile Crescent. After the departure of the French, power alternated between various civilian politicians, such as Jamil Mardam and Shukri al-Quwatli, and a larger number of military leaders (Husni Zaim, al-Hinnawi, Shishakli and last, but in the background, that *eminence grise* al-Sarraj). By their activities no less than five *coups d'état* succeeded one another in Syria between 1949 and 1954. The protagonists in turn won and lost power (and in more than one case life also) with the typical methods of military demagogy, reciprocally accusing one another of treason and tyranny.

The questions at issue—ostensibly at least—were the great problems of the political orientation of Syria, for or against the 'Greater Syria' of the Hashemite projects, for or against American economic aid, for or against the British proposal for a unified Middle East defence command and, in the final analysis, for or against one or the other of the two great world blocs. Choice between these alternatives was influenced by urgent economic and social considerations, such as the great poverty of the country, its need of public works and the restless activity of the parties, amongst whom, perhaps more than in any other country of the Arab Near East, Communism was gaining a foothold. In 1957 Communist pressure became so evident, and so strong was the fear that the rival group of Khalid al-Azm would take the initiative, that as a last resource President Shukri al-Quwatli was induced to accept and almost to solicit the union of Syria with the Egypt of Nasser.

So closed a decade which certainly did no honour to the wisdom and political maturity of the Syrian ruling class. It had showed itself incapable of maintaining the autonomous character of the country in peace and liberty and was reduced to subordinating its own land to another Arab country under the aegis of a dictatorship. The sacrifice of the martyrs of 1915 should in truth have deserved a better fate for Syria.

The history of the Lebanon, on the other hand, was more peaceable. Constitutional democracy developed smoothly until the spring and summer of 1958, when a long internal crisis threatened to become international. The civil war which raged there during those months originated outside the country with the opposition to President Chamoun and calmed down after the election of his successor, General Chehab. It was not, however, limited to purely personal rivalries. It became entangled both in the expansionist plans of the United Arab Republic and in the Iraqi-Jordanian crisis which was going on at the same time. According to some, the landing of American marines (July to October) asked for by President Chamoun only complicated the situation, but more probably it helped the settlement of Lebanese internal problems. But tremors of unrest are still evident in a land which for long has been one of the most peaceful in the Near East and is now troubled not only by its own problems but by all those which it shares with the whole of the Fertile Crescent.

While Saudi Arabia digests its oil and the profits thereof, without displaying any appreciable symptom of evolution from the patriarchal absolutism that governs it, on the other side of Sinai the Arab world has been living through a most dramatic and precipitous phase of its evolution. But before recalling the main events in Egypt which have determined all the more recent history of the Near East, we must register the birth, to the south of Egypt, of the latest sovereign state outside the Maghreb to associate itself with the Arab community of peoples: the Sudan. Full independence, proclaimed on 1st January, 1956, has been the culmination of a long three-cornered struggle between the two partners in the condominium of 1899 and the Sudan—at the outset simply the object of the struggle, but now a free entity, thanks to that very rivalry. Well before her recent expansionist phase Egypt had cast eyes on the Sudan, conquered in the time of Mohammed Ali and later reconquered, after Gordon and the Mahdiyya, to become a mere dependency of the British Empire. Recent Egyptian propaganda treats the Sudan as genuinely Arab and an integral part of the supposed unity of the Nile Valley.

In reality its northern part is of Moslem faith, Arab language, culture and, *lato sensu*, Arab origin, while to the south Negroid strains, primitive faiths and heathen culture prevail. The more civilized north has naturally taken the lead over the south, but the pro-Egyptian party (the Ashiga, or blood-brothers, with a programme of union) was opposed by an autonomous movement favoured by the British (the Umma Party) which finally prevailed. The title 'King of Egypt and of the Sudan' assumed by Farouk in 1951, just as he was about to lose the crown of his ancestors, remained a one-sided affirmation of an old Egyptian hope; and when events provided another solution for the Sudan, Egyptian nationalism was by then too absorbed in other great problems to be able to make any effective opposition.

An Arab republic with certain original constitutional features has thus appeared in the Upper Nile Valley and has assumed international status, accepting purely technical and cultural aid from her two not disinterested former tutors, Great Britain and Egypt. In November 1958 a bloodless *coup d'état* suspended normal constitutional life in the Sudan and placed the power in the hands of General Ibrahim Abboud. A military junta (The Supreme Council of the Armed Forces) assumed the government of the country, dissolving all political parties, but declaring and showing itself a jealous guardian of Sudanese independence. Without glossing over the serious problems that the young state has before it, primarily the assimilation and civic advancement of the semi-barbarous South, it is natural to welcome this success for the self-determination of peoples, and to look with sympathy on the process of civilization begun there at the end of the nineteenth century and which now seems to be free both from colonial paternalism and from anti-foreign intolerance.

Egypt had emerged from the Second World War in a position of moral leadership among the Arab states (she had been the promoter of the Arab League), but she too had serious political, economic and social problems to solve. The first aim of all the governments, *Wafdist* or other, who succeeded one another after 1945, was the liquidation of every vestige of foreign influence, which meant primarily the abrogation of the long-obsolete Treaty of 1936 and British withdrawal from the Canal Zone.

Negotiations to that end were frequently opened but Britain was, as always, stubborn and dilatory and a definite agreement was reached only in October 1954, when revolution had already broken out and the Nasser régime was being consolidated. The agreement of 19th October, 1954 really put an end to the period of British military occupation of Egyptian soil which had opened in September 1882 and which, only two years before, had given rise to bloodshed at Ismailia (December 1952). The total evacuation of the Canal Zone was to be completed in twenty months, and this time-limit was adhered to, thus finally restoring to the Egyptians entire sovereignty over their territory. We shall now see how, after the first principle of Mustafa Kamil ('free in our own house') had been realized, the Egyptians interpreted the second, ('generosity to our guests').

Meanwhile life within Egypt itself was seething in turbulent ferment. 'The Moslem Brotherhood' (*al-Ikhwan al-Muslimun*), an extremist group that combined nationalism with religious fanaticism, assumed a leading role in the political life of the post-war period. Its terrorist activities, to which politicians like the Prime Minister, Nokrashy Pasha, fell victim (1948), provoked reprisals and violence in which the founder of the Brotherhood, Sheikh Hassan al-Banna, met his death. On 26th January, 1952 ('Black Saturday') Cairo was for several hours in the power of an anti-foreign mob which gave itself over to arson, destruction and pillage, which the army had neither the power nor the will to prevent.

In those years the Egyptian armed forces were passing

through a difficult material and moral crisis. In 1948, in the improvised campaign against Israel, without training and only half equipped, they had received a thorough beating. At first attempts were made to conceal this (the troops returning from Palestine were welcomed in Cairo as victors) and then to excuse it by making the usual charges of corruption in the higher ranks, defective arms, lack of supplies and similar half-truths. But whatever may have been the reasons for the defeat, it was a serious mistake of the King not to have taken account of the resentment and bitterness of the army, and to have added fuel to the fire by his own dissipations and undue interferences and favouritism. This was nothing new in modern Egyptian history, since all his descendants had regarded themselves as the legitimate heirs of Mohammed Ali, that is to say the absolute masters of the country rather than sovereigns of a constitutional monarchy. But sincere patriotism and disgust at sordid self-interest, especially among the young officer class, could not endure this state of affairs any longer; hence the revolution of 23rd July, 1952.

On that day a group of officers, at first led by General Mohammed Neguib, demanded and obtained without a struggle the abdication and exile from the country of King Farouk, who had long exhausted the popularity of the early years of his reign. He was at first succeeded by his infant son, Fuad II, with a Council of Regency; but on 18th June, 1953, the dynasty of Mohammed Ali was declared at an end and Egypt was proclaimed a republic.

With Neguib as president the real executive power was assumed, as was soon seen, by a junta of young officers, one of whom, Colonel Gamal Abdel Nasser, soon took the leading place. Nasser solemnly announced and inaugurated a great moral, political and social reform of Egypt which involved the dissolution of the parties, a new constitution, limitation of landholdings, abolition of titles, equal distribution of wealth and means of production, and above all, naturally, the fulfilment of nationalist aims in foreign policy.

It remained to be seen whether such a national-socialist

programme (the association of the two adjectives comes spontaneously even without reference to the German precedent) would be carried out after the period of emergency by a return to democratic and parliamentary institutions or by a dictatorship. On this question a conflict began between the moderate Neguib and the extremist group of the Junta led by Nasser, that went through various and dramatic phases in the course of 1954 and ended with the victory of the latter. Between March and November of that year Neguib was little by little excluded from authority, declared a traitor to the revolutionary movement and finally deposed from the Presidency and interned. In the general liquidation of parties was included that of the 'Moslem Brotherhood', which was fairly close in ideological inspiration to the new group in power, but came into conflict with it through obscure personal rivalries and intrigues. An unsuccessful but providential attempt to assassinate Nasser gave an excuse to liquidate it. So from the end of 1954 the young colonel, having put his general under lock and key found himself and his group masters of the Egyptian state.

The machinery of demagogic totalitarianism was thenceforward set in motion by methods well known to the West and to a great extent learnt from it. A new constitution launched in January 1956 conferred on the President (naturally Nasser) vast powers on the model of presidential republics. But the spirit counts more than the form, and there is no doubt that the spirit of the new Egyptian régime is authoritarian, unwilling to bind itself by any law, internal or international. All civil and political liberties, even if not nominally revoked, disappeared, the parties were forbidden, the Press gagged and every movement of discontent from above or from below harshly repressed (in 1953 the workers' agitation by Kafr al-Zayyat was punished by imprisonment and the gallows); the régime drew a semi-mystical justification and authority from contact with the people (who approved in docile plebiscites) and from the conviction, doubtless in some cases sincere, that it was 'working for the good of the country'. This soon became evident within the country in extensive programmes of public works. At the same time legal and administrative action and police persecution eradicated every activity by and the very possibility of existence for foreigners in Egypt ('generous towards our guests . . .'). The work of a century and a half of the European colonies in the Nile Valley, the source of wealth, prosperity and progress not only to themselves but to the country as a whole, was sacrificed to intolerance and resentment.

But the outstanding fruits of such a totalitarian régime are usually to be found in foreign policy and it was here that the Egyptian adventure impinged most dramatically on the international situation. We have already spoken of the agreement reached in 1954 for the total evacuation of Suez, which the new government inherited as a result of the thirty-year-old struggle of its predecessors, primarily the discredited *Wafd*. The British evacuation of the Canal had scarcely been completed in the agreed term of twenty months before the Egyptian dictator unexpectedly nationalized that vital artery of international communications, thus opening the most eventful chapter of recent Mediterranean history.

The legal factors in the controversy are as follows: first, the contract of the Concession of 22nd February, 1866, between the Khedive Ismail and the Canal Company. According to the Egyptian thesis, from this results the unequivocally 'Egyptian' status of the company itself, which is regulated by the laws, and subject to the exclusive sovereignty, of the Egyptian state. Therefore, runs the argument, the nationalization of the Canal can be considered as a straightforward internal action undertaken by Egypt, being both legal and internationally unassailable. The second factor is the Constantinople Convention of the 29th October, 1888, whereby the European Powers and Turkey (which must here be considered as representing Egypt) guaranteed free use of the Canal, in wartime as in peace, with neutral status and forbidden as a base for warships. Egypt maintained that the Convention directly empowered her own government to permit transit to the ships of all nations (with the obvious exception of those with whom she was in a state of war) rather than merely giving her the duty of authorizing another foreign organization to locally govern the traffic.

The countries using the canal (France and Great Britain, in fact) put forward an opposing argument, and held that the 1888 Convention had been violated by the nationalization of the Canal. For, as Article 2 of the Convention stated that the contracting powers had taken into account the agreement concluded between the Khedive and the Company, the Franco-British point of view was that the conditions attached to the initial agreement had become an integral part of the Convention. Therefore, Egypt could not rightfully abrogate it unilaterally to the prejudice of the contracting nations. Moreover, by virtue of Article 8 of the Convention the diplomatic representatives of the signatory nations in Egypt were commissioned to supervise the fulfilment of the obligations laid down, and were empowered, if necessary, to request the Egyptian government to remove any obstacles that might be put in the way of free international navigation. This, according to France and Great Britain was equivalent to an effective 'internationalization' of the Canal. Thus, even if Egypt could legitimately have dissolved the Company, she would first have had to warn all the nations involved, and then have come to an agreement with them for the creation of another body capable of continuing the activities of the defunct organization. Finally, on the European side it was pointed out that although the Canal Company was an Egyptian organization, its creation and headquarters, its capital and directors, its officials and its activities had all displayed a markedly international character in the course of nearly a century. Its whole function was in fact an international one, and was not something that the Egyptian government could unilaterally cease to recognize.

These two conflicting theses of international law can be discussed and interpreted in various ways, but if we remove judgement from the purely juridical level to the political and moral sphere there can be no doubt of the ruthlessness of the Egyptian dictator himself; by the usual method of a *fait accompli* he had finally settled a matter involving not only the indisputable rights and interests of his own country, but also the solemn rights and interests of others.[1]

It may be instructive to recall that twenty years before, and by quite other methods, Turkey, also a nationalist state, had reasserted her sovereign rights over a part of her territory which was also of great international importance, the Straits. Whatever differences may be found between the two situations, the most serious and significant is the difference in conduct of the two dictators: the Turk desirous of reaching an agreement internationally and peaceably accepted at Montreux, the Arab playing a game of bluff and throwing his gesture like a challenge in the face of those who felt they had just settled a knotty and thankless problem.

The details of the Suez crisis are briefly as follows: Nasser proclaimed the nationalization of the Canal (July 1956); France and Britain replied first by protests and offers of negotiation and then (October 1956) by military action synchronized with an Israeli offensive in the Sinai peninsula. An Anglo-French force disembarked at Port Said. The Egyptians blocked the Canal. But the slowness of the operations, partly for military but even more for political reasons, deprived the Anglo-French action of any real efficacy. The open disapproval of America and the Soviet threat of immediate intervention led to second thoughts by the two Western powers and the evacuation of Egyptian territory in December 1956. Later, successive direct negotiations between Egypt and the Suez Canal Company, which meant in effect France and Britain, led the two powers to recognize the *fait accompli* of nationalization and left them with only the jeers earned by their abortive intervention.

Certainly, though there was outright provocation by the Egyptians, the principles and methods of the Anglo-French reaction seem no less deplorable, in trying to retrieve the situation by a unilateral and ill-executed *coup de force* that only the widest international sanction could have justified. Mistaken both in pure law and as political opportunism, the action of

[1] It should not be forgotten that the Canal Concession would in any case have have come to an end in 1968.

October–November 1956 proved equally futile in practical effect. It was a classic case of disregard for the Machiavellian maxim that enemies must be either flattered or eliminated but never unnecessarily offended.

The result of that episode, which in the autumn of 1956 seemed as if it were leading the whole world to the brink of a third world war, was the victory of Nasser. He had bluffed audaciously, profiting by the disunion and indecision of others and aided by the anti-interventionalist attitude of the power which, during those very same days, intervened so massively in Hungary. In the eyes of the Arab world, France and Britain had seemed to revert to the old arrogance, not yet forgotten, of the West towards the East. The Egyptian dictator, who had been within a hairsbreadth of collapse after military defeat by the Israelis in Sinai and by the Anglo-French forces in the Canal Zone, was at the end of it all still in the saddle, wearing the halo of defender of his country and of right. The Arabs had a fresh proof that colonialism was not yet dead, the Canal remained blocked for a year, and petrol became more expensive for colonialists and anti-colonialists alike. Nothing more miserable could be imagined as the tragi-comic epilogue to the enterprise of de Lesseps (whose statue on the Canal was meanwhile blown up with dynamite), ninety years after it had been inaugurated with the solemn declaration by Ismail that Egypt was henceforth a part of Europe. Ismail's successor, the colonel, showed his countrymen and the world that Egypt, reinvigorated by injections of totalitarianism, was now capable of holding her own with Europe. The next step was bound to be the revival of the pan-Arab ideal.

The final, political result of the Suez Crisis was the substantial and, we may say, the formal capitulation of the two European powers. By agreeing with Egypt over the amount of the indemnity owing to the Canal Company and its manner of payment, they had in fact recognized the deed of nationalization. The resumption of diplomatic relations (December 1959) marks the definite conclusion of the painful controversy, in which the Western world had shown itself to be divided, aggressive, and impotent.

The Re-awakening of the Maghreb

The Re-awakening of the Maghreb

THE SECOND POST-WAR PERIOD has seen the almost complete emancipation of the Arab Moslem West, the Maghreb, partly thanks to a favourable trend of world events and partly as the natural conclusion to a long and troubled process. The stretch of North Africa west of Egypt has always been felt, by the Arabs of East and West alike, to be an area of the Arab world with special characteristics that distinguish it without detaching it from the rest. The Arab conquerors had superimposed themselves on the indigenous peoples and cultures (Libyans and Berbers) who rapidly assimilated Islam and the Arab language and culture, but in their turn added to them traces of their own psychology, customs and beliefs. Though the Arab West enjoyed its periods of power and splendour (of which the peak was in medieval Spain), the level of civilization remained as a whole lower than in the East, as is confirmed by the modern history of the corsair states of Barbary. Then in the nineteenth and twentieth centuries all Northern Africa was opened up to European colonization as a territory ripe for long-term civilizing (and corresponding profits), but more recently the onflow of world crises and the Arab revival in the East has reacted with unsuspected speed and effect on the Maghreb, liberating three-quarters of it from European colonization in little more than a decade.

Italy and France were the protagonists of this penetration into, and equally of the subsequent rapid evacuation from North Africa. Italy, the latest comer, was the first to be expelled. If Italy did little or nothing for the political education of the Libyan people (the real reconquest of the country, after 1922, was carried out when the colonizers had themselves lost their liberty and certainly could not give to others what they no longer possessed), there remains to her honour the very considerable modernization and material advancement of the

country, its urban development and a vast agricultural transformation and improvement, later interrupted and ruined by
the war, all leading to a higher living standard for the Libyan
people themselves. This deserves to be remembered, in the
interests of truth, as much as the repressions of General
Graziani, and should not be completely forgotten by the Libyan
upper class that was created during the decades of Italian
occupation.

The North African liberation movement was greatly spurred
by the unexpected and little-earned independence of Libya,
but in any case, as we watch the disastrous rearguard action
being fought by France to slow down the disintegration of
her North African Empire, we realize that Italy can console
herself with the thought that she has been spared much
else by her providential misfortunes in the Second World
War.

The rest of the contemporary history of the Maghreb is the
drama of the far more bitter and eventful liquidation of the
French colonies. The work of France in North Africa deserves
full recognition from even the most convinced (but still
rational) adversary of colonialism as far as material civilization
and, here no less than in the Levant, spiritual awakening and
enlightenment are concerned. The Arabs who fought, and are
still fighting, for the emancipation of the Maghreb in Tunisia,
Morocco and Algeria, imbibed French culture with their
mothers' milk, more fully even than the Arab nationalists of the
Lebanon and Syria. In French schools and through the French
Press and propaganda, they learnt about the Revolution and the
principles of 1789, the French contribution to the history of the
human spirit, and the civilization of the world. Some of these
men, even leaders of the Algerian insurrection, do not speak
or properly understand Arabic, so radical has been their
cultural assimilation by France. Some have shed their blood
for France in two world wars, before shedding it in an opposing
cause for the liberation of their own country. But the call of
nationality—though probably all in all the most balanced
nationalism in the Arab world, and more disposed towards

co-operation than any in the East—has been strong enough to offset their education.

Some of the motives behind the French opposition to Algerian independence was worthy and noble—the conscious-ness of a great work of civilization still to be done and of the potential benefits from Franco-Maghreb co-operation; but alongside these there is still also an old blind nationalist pride and powerful if less openly acknowledged economic interests: the great and small landholdings, the industrial investments and the glittering new prospects of Sahara oil. All these factors lead straight to the heart of the still unresolved Algerian drama; but first we must outline the process of Tunisian and Morrocan emancipation. These cases have certain features in common: a sullen French opposition, concessions alternating with periods of repression, sincere attempts at co-operation by civil servants alternating with *coups de force* by military commissioners, appeasement missions accompanied by arrests and deportations. Even at the very last moment a vain attempt was made to write old-fashioned military-base clauses into the agreement, but finally the treaties of independence were actually signed, and the last page of the history of direct French dominion was written.

In both Tunisia and Morocco the survival of a native state, even though under protectorate, with a dynasty and national tradition, provided a lever for resistance and later for revolt. In Tunis the Beys, who succeeded one another from 1881 to the Second World War, adapted themselves peaceably enough to the Protectorate, until al-Munsif (1942–3) who took an openly nationalist point of view and, in the winter of 1942–3, threw in his lot with Germany. But much earlier, in 1920 and 1933 respectively, two parties of revolt arose in Tunis: the 'Destour' (which in Arabic means Constitution, whence it may be called the 'Constitutional Party') and the 'Neo-Destour' which differed from the first and more traditionalist party by a more modern conception of political struggle. Amongst the leaders of the latter party, which save for brief intervals has always represented the active wing of the liberation movement, were fervent

Tunisian patriots like Habib Thamir (died in 1950), Salah ben Youssef and Habib Bourguiba, destined to become the leader of independent Tunisia. Bourguiba was one of those whose whole being was saturated with French culture, free from fanatical rancour against the West and disposed to wide measures of co-operation, but absolutely firm in the interests of national independence.

French policy was cautiously liberal (political and administrative reforms in February 1945, an emphasis on cultural relations with the founding of the *Institut des hautes études tunisiennes*, and above all the experiment in conciliation under the Resident Perillier, 1950–2), but not without recourse, at various times, to force. In 1943, after Tunisia had been reoccupied by the Allied forces, the France of de Gaulle hastened to deport and exile the Bey, al-Munsif, who died a few years later, his gamble on the losing side not having been very wise for the emancipation of his country. His successor, al-Amin (1943–57) who was to be the last of his dynasty, was by no means so meek towards the protectors as the campaign for his deposition made him out to be, and many times in the tug-of-war that lasted from 1950 to 1955 he stood up with firmness and dignity to the demands of the Residents, from de Hautecloque to Marshal Juin.

The blackest page of French rule in Tunisia was in January-February 1952, when serious disorders broke out all over the country after the arrest of Bourguiba and other nationalist and Communist leaders. Their crime was to have instigated an appeal by the Tunisian government to the United Nations, and a merciless repression followed which filled Cape Bon with blood for a week. Fresh reforms followed under the Bakkush government, and fresh attempts to appeal to the United Nations, which were rejected or evaded by France on the pretext that it was an 'internal matter'. The situation was only finally relieved in the summer of 1955, when Mendès-France had the generosity and intelligence to recognize the now irresistible movement towards independence in North Africa (or at least in Tunisia and Morocco, which by great good fortune had not become

French 'metropolitan territory' as had Algeria), and the courage to declare that France 'could not condemn these peoples for the ideals that she herself had taught them'.

The final step was taken and what remained was only a diplomatic epilogue; the Franco-Tunisian negotiations culminating in the declaration of independence on 20th March, 1956 which abrogated the Treaty of Bardo and put an end to the Protectorate. Tunisia saluted Bourguiba as its liberator, a brave fighter who possessed the sense of moderation and generosity (and therefore ended by breaking with the extremist Salah ben-Youssef, who fled the country), and enthusiastically entrusted its destinies to him a little later (July 1957). He abolished the rule of the dynasty of the Beys and proclaimed a republic, of which he, naturally, assumed the presidency as well as the government. The last logical consequence, the withdrawal of troops that France sought by every means to delay, was the subject of a bitter dispute up to the summer of 1958. It was ended by the agreements of that year which provided for a gradual but complete withdrawal save for the base at Bizerta.

The Tunisian leader, one of the most likeable and humane men of the Arab revival, then found himself embarked on an ambivalent policy of co-operation with France, towards which he had always been inclined for both rational and sentimental reasons, and moral and material support for Algerian independence, the fight for which was to be conducted to a large extent across the Tunisian border. The claims of Arab and Maghreb solidarity, with the Algerian problems as its most thorny point, were affirmed in the Treaties of Friendship with Morocco and Libya (1957) and in vague plans for closer North African co-operation, with or without French participation, as a separate movement from the Arab imperialism in the East that was being developed under the aegis of Nasser's Egypt.

This rivalry between Tunisia and Egypt, that is to say between Bourguiba and Nasser, has, like the present break between Iraq and Egypt, been one of the most serious fissures in pan-Arab unity. There are still no direct relations between the two states, and Tunisia, like Iraq, was not represented at the meeting of the Arab League in September 1959.

The French had been in Tunisia for seventy-five years, but in Morocco for only about forty, or even less if one takes into consideration the fact that full military control of the whole area was achieved only in 1934. The treaty of 30th March, 1912 placed the one Arab country of North Africa that had until then preserved its independence under French 'assistance', for, up to the end of the nineteenth century Morocco had avoided Turkish infiltration both in the days of Ottoman hegemony and of the Barbary States, and had confined every Spanish or Portuguese incursion to small areas on its coasts. The French annexation that began in the early twentieth century with a series of notable international crises and meetings (the Conference of Algeçiras, 1906, the Agadir incident, 1911, and the Franco-German agreement of the same year), was held up by the First World War but resumed after it, under the prudent and enlightened guidance of Lyautey, certainly the most intelligent and therefore, from the native point of view, the most dangerous of the colonialists. He indeed saw and laid down (in, for instance, a confidential report of 1920 that has since been published by the Moroccan nationalists) the necessity for real co-operation between the native authorities and the protecting power if the Protectorate were not to remain a form of words masking direct rule. Lyautey's work went on until 1925, and was devoted to this positive Franco-Moslem co-operation.

Other Residents, his successors, however, soon found Moroccan nationalist opposition on their hands, an opposition which Lyautey had foreseen and tried to forestall by his conciliatory policy. Armed resistance to both the foreign occupiers, France and Spain, was carried on valiantly from 1921 to 1926 by the Riffian leader, Abdul Krim, but in the end he was compelled to bow to European military superiority. During the years after 1930 in which the French military control was being consolidated, political resistance survived and ought to have been met by the French with methods which they did not always want to adopt, or even to admit.

The Re-awakening of the Maghreb

To impose her will on the country France preferred to rely upon Arab-Berber rivalry, playing off the Arabs of the town against the Berber tribes of the interior who with their own language, customs and archaic social structure always acted as a counter-weight to the authority of the central Moroccan government. An outstanding event in this contest was the Sultan's decree of 1930 (the 'Berber *dahir*'), forced on him by the French. Contrary to Moslem canon law, this recognized the jurisdiction of the local Berber courts set up according to customary law, and excited enormous indignation in Arab-Islamic circles in Morocco and abroad.

During the thirties, while the occupation of the interior was being consolidated and an imposing programme of public works, the most striking legacy of French colonization, was being carried out, the first voices of a new-born native nationalism were making themselves heard, no longer merely anti-French, but positively pro-Moroccan. They took form in the 'Requests of the Moroccan People', presented in 1934 by a group of notables to the Sultan Mohammed Ibn Yusuf (ascended the throne in 1927 and still reigning), in which, without going so far as to demand the abolition of the Protectorate, they demanded extensive political and administrative reforms that would give Moroccans a larger direct share in the government of the country. A little later, in October 1937, followed the 'National Pact' of Rabat which can be considered the first formal expression of Moroccan nationalism, at that time personified in the 'Nationalist Party' of Allal al-Fassi. The immediate French response was, as usual, the arrest and exile of the promoters; but the seed was now sown and there was not long to wait for the fruit.

At the time of the Second World War, when Morocco was an Allied base from November 1942, and Moroccan contingents fought alongside the French in the Italian campaign, the Nationalist Party of al-Fassi was merged with the similar 'Popular Movement' of al-Wazzani, and became in January 1944 the united 'Party of Independence' (*Hizb al-Istiqlal*) which thenceforward uncompromisingly carried on the struggle for complete liberation. This lasted twelve years and ended almost at the same time as that of Tunisia with the full victory of the Moroccans and of their sovereign, who knew better than the Tunisian Bey how to give up his old authority while at the same time reaping advantage from the new.[1] Mohammed Ibn Yusuf (later to be known as Mohammed V) had stressed the right of the Moroccan people to unity, and so implicitly to independence, thus putting himself at the head of the liberation movement as long ago as 1947 in internationalized Tangier, which welcomed him with great demonstrations of loyalty.

France tried to hold back the movement by a mixture of concessions and force. Marshal Juin, suddenly sent as new Resident to Rabat, engaged in a political duel with the Sultan, in which he was aided by, amongst others, the powerful Berber chieftain of the Atlas Mountains, al-Glawi, the symbol of Berber autonomy and feudalism. In the crisis of February 1951, the Sultan was compelled under pressure to repudiate the *Istiqlal*, but this momentary bowing to violence did no harm to his prestige, which France set about enhancing by the halo of persecution. Forced to abdicate in August 1953 he was deported to Madagascar, while his uncle, Ben Arafa, an obsequious instrument of the Residency, was elevated to the throne. This was the last attempt to save the heritage of Lyautey, carried out in a way which he would have condemned and which in any case achieved nothing.

Two years later (November 1955) the exiled Mohammed Ibn Yusuf returned in triumph to his country and his throne; Ben Arafa disappeared into the shadows, el-Glawi bowed in homage to his legitimate sovereign and almost at once discussions opened in Paris for a radical solution of the Moroccan problem.

This was achieved with the agreement of 2nd March, 1956, when the French protectorate came to an end, and the ancient Sherifian Empire once again acquired its independence under

[1] Co-operation with parallel movements in the Maghreb was carried on through 'The North African Defence Front' with which the old exile Abdul Krim was associated, and which united Moroccans, Tunisians, and Algerians and held a 'Congress of the Arab Maghreb' in Cairo in 1947.

the Hasanid dynasty. In the spirit of the times and by the choice of the new European-educated intelligentsia,[1] the medieval monarchy was transformed, at least on paper, into a modern state; but the actual realization of these plans is something that still lies in the future. On the plane of present realities, it is important to stress the revival, not only of independence, but of Moroccan unity.

The end of the French Protectorate was in fact followed by the end of that of Spain, who wisely renounced a long-hopeless defence of their zone, the preservation of which had in the past been the cause of so much bitterness and sacrifice. The Madrid agreement of 7th April, 1956 sanctioned the end of the Spanish Protectorate and the agreement of Tangier on 29th October of the same year marked the end of the international régime there. The usual haggling over the military withdrawal remained, but even this was settled for both zones (summer 1958).

But as appetite comes with eating, the revived Moroccan Empire was already advancing claims to the vast area of French West Africa which in November 1960 became the Islamic Republic of Mauretania. Whatever may be the destiny of this emerging expansionism of the Maghreb,[2] history now records the end of colonialism in this still backward country, with its vast potential resources. Morocco has won its international status and is preparing itself for modernization under the guidance of an enlightened monarch and of a young ruling class which owes its best features to what it has assimilated from the West.

Tunisia, Libya and Morocco are today sovereign states, members of the Arab League and of the United Nations. The chain of free Arab states in the Maghreb, indeed the whole Arab chain over two continents, is broken only between Bône and Oujda by the most conspicuous survival of the old colonialism:

[1] The leader of the *Istiqlal*, Allal al-Fassi, has already been mentioned; also taking part were Sidi Bekkai, Ahmed Balafrej, Abdul Krim, ben-Jallun, and others who later became members of the first cabinets after independence. The modernizing tendency has been endorsed in the royal family, where a daughter of the Sultan has made herself the prime mover for feminine emancipation and the abolition of the veil.

[2] There is still doubt how far the effective authority of the Sultan's government really reaches in the immense and primitive Moroccan hinterland.

Algeria. Unlike Tunisia and Morocco, but more like Libya, Moslem Algeria cannot boast of any long and deep-rooted native state-tradition earlier than European penetration. In the past the present territory of Algeria formed part of several Maghreb states to the east and west, and the appearance of unity achieved in the Ottoman-Barbary period broke up after the disappearance of the Deys in 1930, to be created anew by French conquest and administration.

For the whole of the second half of the nineteenth and the first years of the twentieth century, France was here able to develop to the full her greatest colonial experiment in North Africa, without the formal incumbrance of native authorities or international complications; and a vast immigration of settlers from the mother-country soon modified the demographic character of Algeria (which did not happen, save in a very small way, in Tunisia and Morocco). Alongside the Arab population a class of African Frenchmen was created which was rooted to the soil not only by material interests but by the traditions and affections of several generations. Today statistics show more than a million such Frenchmen in Algeria among eight or nine million Arab Moslems. This is a really embarrassing ratio, neither the parity between the Christian and Moslem elements that exists in the Lebanon, nor the shattering native majority over European minorities in other African countries.

It is just that all this should be recalled in order to explain the gravity and the complexity of the problem which the rise of Algerian nationalism has posed for France, cutting into all her other political, economic, demographic and social problems. The magic word 'integration' which we use so much ought in fact to have been the aim of a long-term Algerian policy for several decades past, from the time of the first stirrings of a national consciousness and of the first native claims. It would have meant the gradual but effective advancement of the Arab population to the political and civil rights and duties of French Algerians, to parliamentary representation, and to all the privileges and advantages of the European minority. But the logic that argues that advantages shared by many are reduced in value, and that privileges descending from a minority to a majority cease to be such, renders a policy of assimilation too opposed to the interests, if not of France, then at least of many Frenchmen on both sides of the Mediterranean to be sincerely proposed or faithfully carried out.

The policy that France followed with the Arabs of Algeria in order to keep them weak was the same that had for so long been followed in Tunisia and Morocco; concessions of form rendered valueless in substance, words and promises contradicted by facts. Everywhere in the Arab world, the consciousness of rights and national claims was rising and with it that aversion for the West which, especially in Algeria, the West would have been able to avoid only by the most generous invitation to the native peoples to participate in its own spiritual and material wealth. The result of this failure has been the present Algerian impasse, an open sore in the body of France, which it is still impossible to see how and when it can be healed.

The beginnings of the Algerian nationalist movement can be traced back to the first post-war period, to Algerians who did not deny the superiority of European culture and civilization but only desired equal access to its benefits for their co-nationals; such were, at least at first, al-Masali (the 'Messali' of the French), one of the first leaders of the 'North African Star', nationalist and Communist in his views, and Ferhat Abbas, today the leader of the nominal 'Algerian Government in Exile', but who began his career as a moderate, imbued with French culture and French rhetoric and sceptical of the possibility of an Algerian nation and country. Men with more extreme aims emerged in the twenty-year inter-war period, such as Ibn Badis, founder of the traditionalist 'Association of the *Ulema* of Algeria' (1931).

Later stages of the nationalist movement were the foundation by al-Masali of the 'Algerian Popular Party' (1937) and the 'Manifesto of the Algerian People' (1943) drawn up by Ferhat Abbas, thenceforward devoted to more radical views, and co-founder with al-Masali of the 'Friends of the Manifesto and of Liberty' in 1944. The idea of this movement was still to turn the constitution of Algeria into 'an autonomous republic federated with a revived French republic, anti-colonial and anti-imperialist'; an ideal which, until very recently, at least a part of French public opinion would have found acceptable and even desirable as a solution of the Algerian problem. But the France of the liberation replied with the dissolution of the movement and the arrest of Ferhat Abbas. The year 1945 also saw the bloodiest incidents before the general revolt of 1954, when the insurgents of Setif and Ghelma were put down by a savage military reprisal that cost at least eight or ten thousand victims. The next year, Ferhat Abbas founded the 'Democratic Union of Algerian Manifesto' (UDMA) which together with the 'Movement for the Triumph of Democratic Liberties' (MTLD) constituted the principal nationalist group up to the insurrection.

Under the pressure of these ideas and these events, France introduced the Organic Statute for Algeria in September 1947. In the eyes of its promoters, this was to give the broadest and most equitable satisfaction to native aspirations compatible with those of the French colonists; Algeria ceased to be a dependency of the mother-country and was assimilated into metropolitan France and divided into three *départements*, while French citizenship was granted to all Algerians with, however, a distinction between citizens of 'French status' and citizens of 'personal status' (the latter being the great majority of the Arab Moslems of Algeria); a local Algerian Assembly was set up, with primarily administrative powers, elected by a double electoral college of the two above-mentioned distinct categories, that is to say the mass of the French Algerians with the 'assimilated' Arabs, and the Moslem Arabs, each with an equal number of seats (30 and 30, elected respectively by one and a half million electors representing the one million two hundred thousand Europeans).

Notwithstanding this unequal division intended to prevent the great Arab majority being reflected in the Assembly, the 1947 Statute was regarded by the local French officials and colonists as a dangerous and unacceptable concession to native nationalism, and the elections that followed were stage-managed in such a way as to ensure the return of representatives docile to French interests even in the native college of the Assembly. This unworthy sabotage and annulment *in loco* of the partial concession granted by the Statute marked the final disillusionment of the Algerian nationalists and their adoption of more extreme measures leading to armed insurrection.

The insurrection exploded, on the pre-arranged date of 1st November, 1954, under the control of a Revolutionary Committee of Unity and Action, with volunteer forces efficiently organized (FLN: National Liberation Front).[1] Supplied from secret bases and reinforced via Tunisia and Morocco, the rebels at first held the eastern zone of mountains and then involved the whole of Algeria in a bloody guerrilla war which the French regular army, with massive use of men and equipment, has not yet succeeded in subduing.

The terrible wastage of blood and property that the guerrilla war has cost France (according to current figures, a daily expense of about two thousand million francs) has not been the only price paid for the stubborn old spirit of colonialism and the forces that bind it to French political life. The moral damage suffered by the Republic has been all the more serious because it has weakened its prestige in the new Maghreb states and in those of the Arab world in general. In particular the shameful methods of torture and repression employed, methods reminiscent of the Gestapo, have shocked the better part of public opinion even in France itself. When firmness in high places seemed to waver on the Algerian problem and there was some possibility of negotiations with the rebels, even of a complete capitulation as in the war in Indo-China, the colonists and the army forced the hand of the mother-country and, by the sedition of May 1958, brought de Gaulle to power by the threat of civil war, thinking in this way to bar the way to any solution that involved 'renunciation'. In reality, the victory over the

[1] The FLN comprises the majority of the rebels; a dissident combat group is the MNA (Algerian Nationalist Movement) led by al-Masali, exiled in France.

defenceless parliamentary democracy of Paris was obtained at a considerably lower cost than a military victory over the rebels would have been, even had it been possible.

There remains the hope, primarily in de Gaulle himself and certain groups to whom moderate European and Arab elements in Algeria might be able to rally, of a political solution that would isolate and little by little reduce the intransigence of the rebels and bring a pacified Algeria back to co-operation with France within some federal association (this had been the Algerians' own programme ten years before). However much this may be in contrast to the ideals of absolute independence which all the rest of the Arab world has adopted, there seems no reason to exclude it *a priori* when the special historical and demographic conditions of the country are considered. But what is certain is that any kind of non-extremist solution presupposes a sincere and effective approach to the natives, not with stage-managed mass demonstrations but facing the real facts and without regard for the interests of those who inspired and directed the sedition of May 1958. Until this readiness to compromise is reached there seems no way out of the dilemma; the best reformist intentions of the new French régime are impotent to act and the chances of a peaceful solution more uncertain than ever.

De Gaulle's declaration of September 1959 on the future of Algeria seemed to offer a new solution to the whole problem.[1] For the first time the responsible head of the French nation had recognized the fact that the destiny of Algeria should depend on the freely expressed choice of her own people. They were to be offered three solutions: complete '*integration*' with 'Metropolitan France', autonomy within the framework of a French '*Commonwealth*', or total independence with secession. Although

[1] De Gaulle's declaration on Algeria of 16th September, 1959, referring the future of the country to the free choice of the local inhabitants (French and Moslem) explicitly lays down three possibilities: total secession, complete integration with France, or Algerian self-government federated with and supported by France. The great question in this just and humane proposal (which has already aroused the suspicions of the ultra-French no less than among the Arab extremists) is how far liberty of choice will be effective within the time fixed by de Gaulle, which is at the latest four years after the military pacification of the country.

De Gaulle deprecated this last choice even as he proposed it, as being both absurd and ruinous for Algeria, the very fact that such a thing had been mentioned, if only in theory, was a great step forward in the direction of negotiations with the rebels. So much so, in fact, that the 'Algerian Provisional Government in exile' was obliged to consider the proposals, and admit, though with due reservations, the possibility of a dialogue on these terms. Similarly, the admission that secession might be a possible solution excited violent feelings of bewilderment and apprehension among French colonial and military circles. They felt that the whole legitimate foundation for their permanency in Algeria was being threatened.

In an interview in January 1960, General Massu clearly expressed the perplexity and mistrust harboured by the army towards the new political line that was being taken by the Head of the State, who owed his rise to power to the extremists' revolt of May 1958 in Algeria. When Paris recalled and disavowed Massu, Algiers again tried to force the hand of the Government by exploding into open revolt. From 24th January to 1st February, armed bands of citizens and soldiers in the Algerian capital openly defied the legal authority of the city and of the mother-country, in an attempt to force the abandonment of the declared principle of self-determination. The army showed itself hesitant in its attitude towards the revolt, and in its final suppression. Finally, after days of anxiety and almost comic uncertainty, De Gaulle spoke to the army and the nation over the radio and succeeded in reasserting his authority. On 1st February, 1960 the revolt was over, without blood being spilled. Nevertheless, this serious episode indicated how long and difficult was the road leading to a solution of the Algerian crisis. In his September speech, De Gaulle had proposed a time-limit of four years in which to arrive at the final act of referendum. At present, it must be admitted that the probability of attaining a truly humane and democratic solution might yet meet with insurmountable obstacles, but by November 1960 it appeared that the mounting pressures of a year-old war had become too much for France to bear. General de Gaulle told his ministers that he intended to work towards an Algerian republic.

One source of comfort seems certain however, when summing up the still incomplete revival of the Maghreb,[1] and that is that even in Algeria it has developed free from direct international complications and has constituted no serious danger to world peace. This is due in part to the downgrading of France as a power. It is due also to the nature of the struggle itself. It is still in the first phase of national claims and irredentism, it demands freedom without as yet degenerating into rabid imperialism and chauvinism as has happened with the Arabs of the East. And may it be said by one who does not accept the materialist view of history that it is also due to the lack in the Maghreb of those natural sources of wealth that can become the objects of competition and hatred between peoples. The prospects of Sahara oil have already been enough to stiffen French extremism in Algeria. We must thank nature for having been so parsimonious to the Arabs of the West in those ill-omened gifts that menace the Arabs of the East with new trials and new servitude at the moment when they have only just won their freedom and are still unpractised in the wise use of that precious possession.

[1] In this respect Sheikh Shekib Arslan (1869–1946) should be remembered not from the Maghreb but as Druse of Syria, who while in exile at Geneva worked actively as a publicist in favour of the revival of the Arabs and of the Maghreb in particular.

Arab Unity and the Arab Problem

Arab Unity and the Arab Problem

IN THE LAST TWO OR THREE YEARS the problems of the Arab world have leapt to the front of the world scene. A nationalist dictatorship in Egypt, guided by a man of undoubted manœuvring ability and devoid of scruples, has generated a movement towards the union of the Arabs of the East which a few years before would have seemed impossible. After having been within a hairsbreadth of falling during the Suez adventure, Nasser has calculated well the advantage that the Arab cause could draw from the division of the world into two blocs and has relied extensively on this in the successive stages of his programme. Without adhering ideologically to the Eastern bloc, he has used the threat of such adherence to force Western agreement to his plans for Arab unity, advancing from success to success, and meeting with opposition only recently in Iraq, where developments had at first seemed yet another striking success for his policy. The final outcome of his leadership in the Fertile Crescent, cannot be foreseen.

American dissociation from and determined opposition to the Anglo-French action against Suez in the autumn of 1956 gave the final blow to the prestige of the West in its relations with the Arab world, making it appear at the same time aggressive and impotent. To bolster this prestige and to compete with the goodwill that Russia had acquired among the Arab nationalists by her supposed intimidation of the aggressors, America launched the 'Eisenhower doctrine' at the beginning of 1957. This promised economic aid to the countries of the Near East (just after having refused Egypt aid for the great Aswan dam project, which had been the immediate cause of Nasser's nationalization of the Canal), as well as political and military support, if asked for, to protect them from Communism.

These promises, against which Russia protested indignantly, met with a response in the various Arab countries varying according to whether they were interpreted as disinterested guarantees of liberty, attempts at economic-political penetration, or external support for the groups in power in individual states. The Eisenhower doctrine served, however, as a reagent to test the political inclinations of the various countries of the Near East; while Iraq, Jordan and the Lebanon (or more exactly their governments) seemed to line themselves up with the West, Egypt continued her proclaimed policy of equidistance between the two blocs, and Syria showed more and more evident signs of moving towards the Soviet Union.

This process, which developed in the summer of 1957 and for a moment seemed to mean the formation there of a real Soviet satellite, finally ended with the precipitous and spectacular fusion of Syria with Egypt on 1st February, 1958.[1] The motives for this historic agreement which was promoted and almost imposed by the old Syrian statesman Shukri al-Quwatli, should be sought in the fear of a complete sovietization of the country and also in internal rivalries. But it is sure that with the formation of the United Arab Republic (under the presidency of Nasser and with obvious Egyptian preponderance) the thousand-year-old ambition of Egypt for the shores of the Eastern Mediterranean was realized and the first step made towards the unity of the Fertile Crescent, abolishing the partition of states that had been made after the First World War.[2]

The price to be paid for this step, as for all the others that will perhaps follow it, has been the loss of internal liberties in the countries concerned. Instead of parliamentarian and approximately democratic régimes (an approximation usually by default, it would be dishonest to deny) often in reality unstable and corrupt, Egypt and Syria are placed under the 'democratic-presidential' régime of the single party (the so-called 'National Union') in the Assembly (*Majlis al-Umma*), and effectively controlled by an unchecked executive and

[1] The proclamation of 1st February was followed by the referendum of the 21st, the Provisional Constitution (5th March) and the dissolution of the parties (13th March), as had already taken place in Egypt: the principal Syrian party was the national-socialist party of the Baath (Arab revival) which ended by approving the fusion.

[2] On 8th March, 1958, the medieval monarchy of the Yemen was also associated with the United Arab Republic, under the title of 'United Arab States'.

an all-powerful police. How much the more civilized and mature part of the Syro-Egyptian intelligentsia had suffered and is suffering from this régime we cannot say, because every liberty of thought and of the Press has disappeared. But whatever may be the inner thoughts and feelings of a minority, it seems certain that the new régime with its nationalist-demagogic slogans and the success of its pan-Arab policy can count on that support of the masses which is the mystic justification of dictatorships.

From the other of the two camps into which the Arab world seems destined to be split came a decision analagous to the creation of the United Arab Republic (UAR). On 14th February, 1958 the formation of an 'Arab Federation' was announced in Baghdad and Amman which, without destroying the autonomous character of the two kingdoms of Iraq and Jordan, bound them in a federal bond under Iraqi control and brought about plans for the unification of foreign policy, the army and the currency. In many ways it recalled the spirit of the Arab revolt, proclaimed thirty years before by the Sherif of Mecca, common great-grandfather of the two Hashemite sovereigns. The two young sovereigns had certainly every right to regard their family pact as simply a continuation of the original movement for Arab liberation and union, the more so as one of the last survivors of that dawn, the proven politician Nuri al-Said, was still at the helm of Iraq.

Thus the two formations, Syro-Egyptian and Iraqi-Jordanian, far from being able to merge into a single higher and final union, faced one another like rivals, and only a trial of force could have tested their respective solidity. But the pro-Western policy of Nuri al-Said, whose most fateful act had been the Iraqi adhesion to, and even initiative for, the Baghdad Pact three years before, had for some time past alienated the sympathies of the more ardent Arab nationalists, who now placed their trust in quite other men and movements.

The crisis broke out in the summer of 1958, appearing first in the imbroglio of the Lebanon civil war. In May, after the murder of a publicist opposed to President Chamoun, the opposition forces entered the field in a sort of guerrilla war, showing themselves as incapable of finally taking over power as the government showed itself incapable of a rapid and radical repression. While the pro-Western leanings of the governing classes were undoubted, those of the rebels did not appear so clear, at least in foreign policy (whence the opinion in international circles that this was a purely internal crisis). The suspicion, however, was obvious that the rebellion was being nourished from outside, that is from the neighbouring United Arab Republic, and already a counter-stroke was being considered by the Baghdad Pact countries either in the form of intervention or at least of aid for the 'legal' Lebanon, when a lightning but certainly long planned *coup d'état* in Iraq completely reversed the situation there and dissolved the ephemeral Iraqi-Jordanian union. A rapid and bloody military rising murdered King Feisal and the whole royal family in Baghdad on 14th July and the Prime Minister, Nuri al-Said, a few days later. Iraq was proclaimed a republic, under the guidance of General Abdul Karim Kassem, who had prepared and directed the insurrection.

While at first the Iraqi revolution seemed a step towards pan-Arab unity inspired by Nasser, the facts corrected and almost reversed this review. The new Iraqi régime was far from disposed to accept Egyptian leadership and tended towards social reforms considerably more advanced than in Egypt, and mainly supported by the extreme left. In the eighteen months after the downfall of the Hashemite dynasty, Iraq went through an extremely precarious phase of her political and social life, with frequent conspiracies, revolts and assassinations (the most serious was the military revolt at Mosul in March 1959 due to pro-Nasser elements, which was suppressed with bloodshed), which Kassem succeeded in overcoming. Meanwhile, external and internal pressure on neighbouring Jordan, where the days of the remaining branch of the Hashemites seemed at first to have been numbered, eased. In the summer of 1958 Great Britain did not hesitate to send parachutists to prop up the last of the Arab states which had remained her friend. But later, due to the courage and ability of the King of Jordan and the subsequent hostility between Iraq and Egypt, the situation there appeared to become more stable.

The Egyptian colonel and the Iraqi general are today the two outstanding figures in an Eastern Arab world,[1] but they face one another in personal and political rivalry.

We must now halt in our account of a historical process that is still in full development, try to draw some conclusions from all that has happened up till now and end with a few sentences of cautious forecast. The Arab revival, which we have seen dawning in the last decades of the nineteenth century inspired by the European-romantic ideal of nationality and the liberal ideal of democracy, has overcome the trials of two world wars and has to a great extent realized its political aims—but with changed ideologies and by changed methods.

Accepting the worst examples of Europe as at one time it accepted the best, it is today inspired by the ideas and methods of the most unbridled nationalism and totalitarianism, a resurrection of the old absolutism with modern techniques. By such ideas and methods it has certainly achieved some out-standing results, liquidating the last vestiges of colonialism over almost the whole area of the Arab world, and playing upon the rivalries of the West to realize its just as well as its less just claims.

The ideal of unity, which goes back to the beginning of the movement for Arab liberation and which was thwarted and frustrated by the West as long as possible, has blazed up anew with unsuspected vigour and has advanced with a speed that it now seems difficult to halt. The federal experiment of the League, that preserved individual sovereignties from opposing interests, having failed, the movement for unity has now taken another course, and from a nucleus of attraction bit by bit absorbs the other parts until a new organism is formed (the 'artichoke method' of Cavour); but there is this difference, that while in the Italian *risorgimento* civil liberties grew parallel with

---

[1] Iraq under General Kassem naturally withdrew from the Baghdad Pact, which changed its name to CENTO (Central Treaty Organization).

the growth of the nation, in the Arab movement today as the one increases, the other diminishes.

The man who today personifies the hopes of the Arabs, and whom the enthusiasm of some of his followers compares with a new Saladin, seems to lack some of the qualities for which that illustrious model was celebrated, primarily good faith and chivalry; but the principle of the end justifying the means is certainly not new, nor is it an Oriental invention. We do not want to deny that certain results achieved today by means that our conscience forbids us to approve can in the end become fruitful and of a worth far beyond that of the men and methods that have made them possible.

The problem that now faces us is no longer Arab only but international: how can this block of Arab states (or the united Arab state of tomorrow) live its own life independently of the colossal groupings that now divide the world? Colonialism has rendered the West irremediably suspect in the eyes of the Eastern peoples and they tend to give more and more credit to Soviet propaganda, which disguises its own plans for penetration behind slogans of liberation (the change of tone is significant between the Afro-Asian Conference of Bandung 1955, equally critical of the West and of the Soviet Union, and that of Cairo in 1957 where anti-colonialist motives and suspicions pointed in one direction only). Once again, in the summer of 1958, the Soviet Union posed as the champion of non-intervention in the internal affairs of the Near East, a Marxist godmother to a non-Marxist Arab family; should this patronage be pressed to its logical conclusion and crowned by the total elimination of the moral and material bonds between the Arab world and the West, what will the consequences be for the Arabs themselves?

To reply to this question two other factors must be borne in mind, factors that we have often glossed over in this essentially political exposition of the Arab revival; one is the economic-social factor which indubitably underlies the national and political problem without however being identical with it (as the Soviet patrons of the Arabs themselves admit, or pretend to admit, when they stress their support for Arab claims without prejudice to their differing social ideologies). The successes of extremist nationalism are in reality largely due, and not in the Arab lands only, to the sullen pressure of the social problem, to the gnawings of need and misery that drive the masses to follow any programme of renewal and subversion that makes promises of higher standards of living. And it has certainly been a major error of the West, America included, to have looked for allies and sympathizers among the satisfied rather than among the hungry in the Near East, among men, classes and movements more interested in the preservation of scandalous social injustices than in their reform. Nationalism has therefore dragged the disinherited and exasperated masses along behind it.

We have already said that Socialism had been the great missing factor in the modern history of the Arab peoples. By Socialism we mean that humanitarian, pacific and pacifist movement which had acted as a counter-balance to the growing power of nationalism in European history prior to the First World War although it was to prove inefficaceous at the decisive moment. In the new Soviet state a doctrine of extreme totalitarianism, both aggressive and bellicose, was substituted for this Western brand of Socialism, which was to be the dynamic force behind the proletariat. When this happened it was able to infiltrate the countries of the Near and Middle East. There, instead of finding its way barred, it often found itself either running in competition or parallel with the extremist doctrines of irredentist nationalism. Although it was difficult to trace this movement in the twenty years between the two world wars, it has revealed itself clearly enough since the end of the Second World War, out of which the Soviet Union emerged with an enormous increase in strength and prestige. Russia was then able to encourage that very same policy of local nationalism in the countries of the East beyond her frontiers that she had crushed at home. At the same time she was able to exacerbate the inveterate hostility that the Afro-Asian peoples felt towards the remnants of European imperialism.

Between the two wars, the Communist parties of the Middle East led a precarious existence. They were persecuted both by the mandatory powers and by the local *bourgeoisie* as they took their first steps towards self-government under European tutelage. But from 1945 onwards, as resentment of all foreign interference grew unchecked, they were able to combine a policy of xenophobia with their radical programme of social revolution. This greatly facilitated the infiltration of Marxist ideology and the economic and political influence of the leader-state (i.e. Russia) throughout the Orient. It is beyond dispute that once these forces joined in the political struggle, they raised delicate problems and brought new complications for the rulers of the latest Arab states. This is particularly apparent in Nasser's Egypt and Iraq under Kassem. In these countries today, there appears to be an uneasy balance in their programmes of nationalism and social progress as they try to resist the pressures from the extreme left. Quite apart from these local fluctuations there remains the fundamental fact that the anti-Western, nationalist revolutions succeeded with the active co-operation of Communism, both internal and external. It is with this that the new nationalist states will eventually have to come to a reckoning.

The final total victory of this nationalism, with the support of the Soviet Union would pose the ultimate problem of internal structure and it would then be seen how the non-Marxist leaders of the Arab world would be able to stand up against the logic of Marxist schemes and to the pressure of the Marxist Empire then at the height of its power. It would also afford the final proof whether it is possible to reconcile the Marxist-materialist viewpoint with the religious factor of Islam, which we have seen retreating ever more and more into the background whenever the nationalist movement prevailed in the Arab revival, but which cannot be said to have been totally eliminated. Whatever may be the tactical truces of the Soviet state with religious faiths, and especially with Islam, it is hard to conceive a more radical contradiction than between Marxist-Leninist materialism and the transcendental and

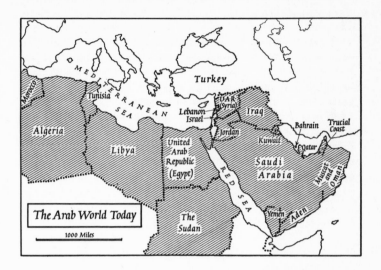

spiritual outlook of Islam. At present these differences are kept in the background, but the day may come when the Arabs will have to choose between their ancestral faith and the word of Moscow.

If, however, the Arabs should succeed in maintaining a 'constructive neutralism' of the Indian type that would really keep them free from direct subordination to either of the two great blocs, then the main problem of an independent Arab world would be its re-education to liberty and its adaptation to modern civilization, two values which have become more and more foreign to it during the harsh struggle for liberation. We mean internal civil liberty, proclaimed on paper in their constitutions but never realized in fact, sacrificed to demagogic authoritarianism, just as it had been in earlier times to absolutism; and by modern civilization we mean political and religious tolerance, philosophical speculation, original scientific research, all of these fields wherein the contribution of the Arabs, as

169

distinct from that of other Oriental peoples, has been little or nothing in modern times by contrast to the splendid pages of their past.

The uncertain and stormy times of today reveal to us a people, once in the van of historical progress, then for long neglected and forgotten, and now reaffirming their existence and their vitality with disconcerting impetuosity, involved in a game with great risks for their own—and our—survival.

Al-haqq yaala, 'Truth prevails', says an Arab proverb—but what is truth? Each nation and each individual may have a different vision of it, and yet a choice has to be made. Many uncertainties and problems remain, but in this book I have offered the only interpretation that convinces me as valid.

Index

Index

Index

ABOUT THE AUTHOR

FRANCESCO GABRIELI was born in Rome in 1904 and is currently teaching at Rome University as Professor of Arabic Language and Literature. Devoted to Arabic and Persian literature, as well as the history of Islam, his scholarship has produced major works in these fields. They include *Il Califfato di Hishâm* (1935) on the Omayyad period, and writings on the ancient poetic tradition of the Arabs. He has also published a history of Arabic literature (second edition, 1956), an account of the Arab chroniclers of the Crusades (1959) and a general survey, *Gli Arabi* (1958). A collection of his essays and other papers appeared as *Saggi Orientali* (1960).

Though Professor Gabrieli's studies have led him into the byways of the specialist, his large and varied output reflects his own political and human standards. He is well acquainted with the Moslem shores of the Mediterranean and during 1955 held a visiting professorship at Algiers University.